youth bible studies

All the King's Men

Faith Weaver™
Youth Bible Studies

www.faithweaver.com

Group
Loveland, Colorado

Group's R.E.A.L. Guarantee to you:

Every Group resource incorporates our R.E.A.L. approach to ministry—a unique philosophy that results in long-term retention and life transformation. It's ministry that's:

This is EARL. He's R.E.A.L. mixed up. (Get it?)

Relational
Because student-to-student interaction enhances learning and builds Christian friendships.

Experiential
Because what students experience sticks with them up to 9 times longer than what they simply hear or read.

Applicable
Because the aim of Christian education is to be both hearers and doers of the Word.

Learner-based
Because students learn more and retain it longer when the process is designed according to how they learn best.

Faith Weaver ™
Youth Bible Studies

Group®

FaithWeaver™ **Youth Bible Studies: All the King's Men**
Copyright © 2001 Group Publishing, Inc.

Visit our Web site: **www.grouppublishing.com**

Credits
Contributing Authors: Tim Baker, Jim Kochenburger, Pamela Malloy, Erin McKay, Kelli B. Trujillo, and Paula Yingst
Editor: Dave Thornton
Chief Creative Officer: Joani Schultz
Copy Editor: Candace McMahan
Art Director: Jeff Spencer
Cover Designer: Jeff A. Storm
Cover Art Director: Jeff White
Cover Illustrator: Jon Flaming
Computer Graphic Artist: Joyce Douglas
Illustrator: Matt Wood
Production Manager: Peggy Naylor

ISBN 0-7644-1180-2
10 9 8 7 6 5 4 3 2 1   03 02 01
Printed in the United States of America.

Contents

Why Do I Need FaithWeaver™ Youth Bible Studies?

A Search Institute study indicates that 86 percent of Christian teenagers do not read the Bible when they are by themselves. There are a variety of reasons, cited in *The Youth Bible*:

"I sometimes don't understand it, so I stop."—Mary in Nebraska

"I'm really confused."—Andrew in Michigan

"I don't know *how* to read the Bible."—Chris in Florida

Part of the reason teenagers find the Bible difficult to understand may be because their exposure to the "whole picture" of God's story has been somewhat limited. Young people often are exposed to the Bible in bits and pieces—a verse here, a passage there—and may never be given instruction about the Bible as a whole—where it came from, how the stories in the Bible fit together, and what the overall meaning of the Bible is. FaithWeaver™ Youth Bible Studies is designed specifically to help students see the "big picture"—starting with the very beginning of the story of God and his people. Through these studies, your youth will not only begin to see how all of the pieces fit together, they'll also see how the Bible's message is very relevant to their lives today.

Essential Components of FaithWeaver™ Youth Bible Studies

Many elements of FaithWeaver Youth Bible Studies bring exciting benefits to your youth. Here are the highlights:

• **Each study is centered around a Key Question that can be answered through the Bible passage and applied to teenagers' lives.** The Key Question each week leads youth to examine Scripture and discover the answer. Teenagers then examine that answer to determine what relevance it has to them. Before the study is over, teenagers will be challenged to take steps toward active application of that Bible principle, weaving their faith into their lives.

• **Each study teaches to multiple intelligences.** Multiple intelligences describe the different ways in which students are smart. For example, some students may have a great deal of kinesthetic intelligence and learn best using hands-on activities. Other students may have more verbal intelligence; these students learn best by processing things through writing or discussing. Because some of your teenagers may be smart in ways that are different from the ways in which you are smart, resist the impulse to skip activities that don't naturally attract you; they may be just what will resonate with some of your students.

• **Each study provides several adaptation tips for younger or older students.** These tips—containing various age-appropriate options for many of the activities—help you customize each study for the needs of your teenagers.

• **Each study contains the historical and cultural context of the Bible story.** The "Historical Context" page provides valuable contextual information about the Bible passage as well as an optional way for students to dig a little deeper into the Bible passage. We've made this a reproducible page so that you may photocopy it and give it to students who want a deeper understanding of the Bible story.

• **Each study includes a "Taking It Home" page.** This page, which you can mail home or distribute during your meeting, provides fun, in-depth activities and discussions to help teenagers explore what they've learned with their families.

• **Each study provides a Faith Journal option with a solid assessment question that will help you discover how well your students are learning as well as help you develop better relationships with them.** At the end of each study, you'll be prompted to have students respond to a "sum-up" question on index cards. You'll collect the cards and take some time during the next week to write affirming responses and comments to what they've written. For example, you may write things such as "I'm glad you gained such a knowledge of God's love during this study" or "Hang in there; God is walking beside you. I'm praying for you." Make these comments as personal and meaningful as you can; it will mean a great deal to your students. At the beginning of the next study, you'll be prompted to return the index cards with your comments on them to your students. It's also a good idea to keep copies of the cards in a notebook or a box so that you'll have an ongoing record of how your students are doing.

Some other options for the Faith Journal cards might be to have students write any prayer concerns they may have or to have them write their own questions about the topic.

If you notice a student response that seems troubling, be sure to touch base with the student sometime right before or after your next meeting. If a student seems to be having problems you're not comfortable handling, ask your pastor or your Christian education director for help.

These innovative, effective learning techniques will transform your classroom into a relational, fun, and caring place for learning. FaithWeaver Youth Bible Studies will help you change the lives of your teenagers and ensure that authentic learning takes place.

About Your Students

These FaithWeaver Youth Bible Studies were written and developed by people who have significant experience working with teenagers. We've designed the studies to be interesting, beneficial, and age-appropriate for youth. As you use the studies to encourage their faith and growth, you might want to keep the following in mind:

• Teenagers' spirituality is, above all, **personal.** They are ready to embrace a more personal relationship with Christ.

• Teenagers' spirituality is **relational.** Relationships with family, friends, peers, and teachers are of high importance to teenagers; they can be encouraged and challenged to examine those relationships in the light of a personal relationship with Christ.

• Teenagers' spirituality is beginning to focus on **future living**. As teenagers look toward their futures, they can be encouraged to consider how their current choices can create their responses to Christ's call in the future.

• Teenagers' spirituality is **multifaceted**. Teenagers hope to discover how their faith can touch and be reflected in all aspects of their lives.

• Teenagers' spirituality is affected by their **physical and mental development**. As their brains develop and their bodies change, teenagers' capacity to think undergoes a dramatic shift, and their world broadens. They become more capable of thinking cognitively and metaphorically.

There's More...

FaithWeaver Youth Bible Studies is just one of the components of Group's Faith-Weaver family of Christian growth resources. This system of resources is composed of three major elements and other supporting materials. The major elements are FaithWeaver Bible Curriculum, KidsOwn Worship™, and FW Friends™. Supporting materials include HomeConnect™ resources for families and Pastor-Connect™ resources for pastors. Any one of these elements can be used without the others. However, using all of them together will help your church's families learn and grow in faith both at church and at home in a way no single book can.

• **FaithWeaver Bible Curriculum**—Designed for use in Sunday school, this portion of the system concentrates on education. Infants through adults cover the same Bible story, learning about it and applying it at appropriate levels for all age groupings. When you use FaithWeaver Youth Bible Studies, you can tie teenagers into a bigger picture of all-church learning.

• **KidsOwn Worship™: FaithWeaver™ Children's Church Kit**—This program includes both preschool and elementary children, with options for joint and separate activities for each. The focus of this element is to learn about worship and to practice it together, while connecting with the story or topic covered in FaithWeaver Bible Curriculum. Here's an opportunity for teenagers to help lead and support children.

• **FW Friends™: Small Groups for Kids**—This program focuses on relationships and service, giving children opportunities to demonstrate their faith in their lives. This is another leadership opportunity for teenagers to mentor younger children.

• **FaithWeaver HomeConnect™**—Two significant resources to help weave faith into life at home are the Adult FaithWeaver Bible Curriculum and the Driving Home the Point weekly page. Within the adult curriculum, a segment written especially for parents and caregivers gives them ways to continue the faith development of their children at home. And the Driving Home the Point weekly page contains devotions, discussions, extra activities, and suggestions to keep the family growing in faith together after leaving the church building.

• **FaithWeaver PastorConnect™**—This element also contains two resources. The first is The Pastor Handbook, which helps the pastor know what's going on in the education program. Using it, the pastor can choose to connect messages or church services with what's being taught. The second resource is a yearly book of children's sermons, *FaithWeaver Children's Messages*, that allows the pastor to present a children's sermon each week that supplements what children are studying in Sunday school.

• **FaithWeaver Internet Link**—Please visit our Web site at www.faithweaver.com to download FaithWeaver materials or to obtain more information about the system.

The FaithWeaver™ Family of Christian Growth Resources

FaithWeaver Bible Curriculum is a tool God will use to change the lives of the children, youth, and adults in your church. Created to be biblically sound, educationally effective, and engaging for every person, FaithWeaver Bible Curriculum will help weave faith into the lives of children and families in your church as no other curriculum can.

Research shows that the most powerful influence on faith development is the conversations about faith that take place in the home. By using all the FaithWeaver Bible Curriculum age levels, you can provide an opportunity for families to study the same Bible passage every week. As toddlers, children, youth, and adults study the same passages—at different levels, of course—students and families will have something to discuss at home.

Using FaithWeaver, your church will be able to weave together Sunday school, children's church, midweek, and adult worship. Or you may want to use just the Bible Curriculum portion of FaithWeaver to further the Christian growth of your church's children and families. It's easy to use, flexible, and powerful! Use it however you want in your ministry to children, youth, or adults. And know that it will positively influence the lives of all who attend.

Worthy of Our Reliance

2 Samuel 5:1-5; Psalm 37

1

David Becomes King

 KEY QUESTION: Why should we rely on God?

 STUDY FOCUS: Students will explore reasons to completely rely on God and will be challenged to rely on him more in their own lives.

KEY VERSE: "God is our refuge and strength, an ever-present help in trouble" (PSALM 46:1).

Psalm 37

A Look at the Study

Study Sequence	Minutes	What Students Will Do	Classroom Supplies
Getting Started	5 to 10	**The Ultimate Thumbless Challenge**—Attempt to do simple tasks without using their thumbs and consider how they often take for granted things they rely on.	Masking tape, pennies, paper, pens, shoes with laces
Bible Story Exploration	10 to 15	**Can't Live Without 'Em**—Discuss manmade objects and the important roles they play in order to explore the countless ways God is our ultimate refuge and strength.	Butcher paper, tape, paper, pencils, marker
	15 to 20	**Why 2 Rely**—Study Psalm 37 and discover the many reasons to rely on God.	Bibles, pens, "Why 2 Rely" handouts (p. 15)
Bible Application	10 to 15	**Commitment Collage**—Evaluate their own patterns of relying on God and make personal commitments to rely on him more.	Bibles, banner from "Can't Live Without 'Em" activity, markers, crayons, CD player, CD of reflective music
	up to 5	**Faith Journal**—Respond in writing to an aspect of the Key Question.	Index cards, pens

Age-Level Insight

One of the most exciting things about being a teenager is the increasing independence that comes with this age. It's a time when society says, "Yes, you're old enough to stay home alone or to baby-sit" and "Yes, you're mature enough to drive" and eventually, "Yes, you're wise enough to vote." Teenagers are no longer completely reliant upon their parents; they're becoming young adults and developing their own opinions and making their own choices.

Teenagers *love* to stretch their wings and fly! "I can do it myself! I have it all figured out!" they often think. In sharp contrast to all of this independence is the idea that human beings need to rely on God, not themselves. It's often difficult for teenagers to find the right balance between establishing their independence and living in total dependence on God. Use this opportunity to show your students how awesome it is to rely on God! Highlight stories of young people in the Bible who did amazing things because of this reliance. (Talk not only about David, but also about Daniel, Esther, and Timothy.) Help your teenagers understand that relying on God will help them to accomplish much greater and more amazing things than they could achieve by relying only on themselves.

NOTES

We begin this quarter of Old Testament studies with the anointing of David as king of Israel. Many years earlier, Israel's first king, Saul, had turned from the Lord, and God had selected David to succeed Saul. For years after that, Saul sought to have David killed. However, David had refused to act against Saul or to become king until he was certain of God's timing. He had lived a difficult life, almost as an outlaw. Now Saul was dead, after being wounded in battle, he had taken his own life. In fact, Saul and three of his sons, including David's friend Jonathan, had died in the same battle (1 Samuel 31:1-6). So the door was wide open for David to become king of Israel.

David didn't rejoice when he learned of the deaths. Instead he and all his men mourned and wept the entire day (2 Samuel 1:1-12). David even wrote a song in honor of Saul and Jonathan, which can be found in 2 Samuel 1:19-27. He was truly saddened that their lives had ended as they did.

David was made king of Judah, but Israel followed Abner, the commander of Saul's army, and made Ish-Bosheth, a son of Saul, king over Israel (2 Samuel 2:1-9). After years of much fighting, intrigue, and bloodshed, Ish-Bosheth was murdered, and the leaders of Israel came to David to make him king over them.

The brief division of the kingdom that had occurred during the war between Ish-Bosheth and David was a foretaste of what was to come. In less than seventy-five years, after the reigns of David and Solomon, Israel and Judah divided into two kingdoms again. However, David's dynasty reigned in Judah for over four hundred years.

David was thirty-seven when he became king over all Israel. He had first been anointed to succeed Saul many years earlier, while still in his teens. After his long, patient wait, David was able to lead Israel to great prosperity, fend off the Philistines, and expand the boundaries of Israel during his reign. David wasn't perfect, but as he relied on God, God rewarded him and Israel with prosperity.

David wrote Psalm 37, which describes his trust in God even when he was surrounded by enemies. In this psalm, David says to "delight yourself in the Lord and he will give you the desires of your heart" (Psalm 37: 4). This could have been the theme of David's life.

Getting Started

The Ultimate Thumbless Challenge

Begin the study by asking your students how many of them are up for an ultimate challenge.

SAY **All you have to do to successfully meet this challenge is pick a penny up from off the ground, sign your name, shake hands with a friend, and untie and tie someone's shoelaces. Does anybody think this will be too tough?**

Here's the catch: You have to do all of these things without using your thumbs!

Distribute strips of masking tape, and encourage students to help each other tape their thumbs snugly against the sides of their hands so their thumbs aren't usable. This may take awhile, but students will laugh as they experience the difficulty of even this simple task.

Once everyone is "thumbless," toss some pennies on the floor, and make paper and pens available as students attempt to master each task without the use of their thumbs. It's a good idea for *you* to wear shoes with laces, just in case no one else does. You might want to add the extra challenge of asking students to try to open a can of soda.

After students have had ample time to "try their hands" at each activity, gather everyone and discuss the following questions.

ASK • **What was the hardest thing to do without your thumbs? Why was it so hard?**
• **What are some other everyday tasks that would be difficult to accomplish without thumbs?**

SAY **It's hard to believe how much we rely on our thumbs! Even though we use them hundreds of times every day, we rarely give a thought to how important they are to us.**

ASK • **Are there any similarities between relying on our thumbs and relying on God in our everyday lives? What are they?**
• **What are some examples of everyday things that, without even realizing it, we rely on God to do?**
• **Why can we rely on God for these things?**

Bible Story Exploration

Can't Live Without 'Em

Tape a very large sheet of butcher paper to the wall. Ask students to raise their hands if they've participated in the following activities.

ASK
- Have any of you ever been bungee jumping?
- How about hiking in a wilderness area?
- Have any of you gone scuba diving? What type of equipment did you use?

SAY Just as we rely on our thumbs to help us accomplish little, everyday tasks, so we also rely on certain objects in extreme situations because our lives depend on them. For example, a bungee jumper *absolutely* relies on that bungee cord! A hiker in the wilderness *absolutely* relies on a compass.

Have students form teams of four to six, and give each team a sheet of paper and a pencil. Ask teams to brainstorm a list of situations in which people absolutely rely on certain objects. Challenge students to think of as many examples as they can in three minutes.

After three minutes, invite teams to share their ideas with the whole group.

SAY In each of these situations, people have specific reasons for relying on certain objects. Now I'd like you to think of at least one unique reason for each object.

Invite students to shout out their ideas as you use a marker to record them in the center of the butcher paper. For example, students might say, "The compass leads them in the right direction" or "The parachute protects them from getting hurt." As you create the list on the banner, word the phrases in a way that could describe God's characteristics—"leads in the right direction" or "protects," for example.

Allow students several minutes to think of unique reasons to rely on all of the objects.

SAY Unfortunately, sometimes these objects let people down. Compasses can get broken, parachutes can fail, and even bungee cords can snap. But God will *never* let us down.

Read aloud the list of phrases you've recorded.

SAY God does all of these things, and more, for us.

Ask students to return to their teams, and invite everyone to share one specific way or time that they relied on God and he responded in one of the ways listed on the banner.

Why 2 Rely

SAY We're about to read about a really important event in David's life: his coronation as Israel's king. David had traveled a long and difficult road to reach this point. He'd been through some really trying times and difficult situations. Yet, through it all, David had relied on God.

ASK
- In what situations had David totally relied on God? How did the situations turn out?

Ask students to look up 2 Samuel 5:1-5 in their Bibles, and ask a volunteer to read the verses aloud.

SAY **God chose David to rule Israel because David had a heart for God; when times were tough, David turned to God as his refuge and strength. And the amazing thing is that even when times *weren't* tough, David still relied on God. God was a crucial part of David's everyday life. David's life can teach us two very important things: *how* to rely on God and *why* to rely on God. Let's take some time to learn from David's own words how and why he relied on God.**

Ask students to rejoin their teams of four to six and to read all of Psalm 37 aloud together, with each student reading at least part of the passage. Make sure that each student has a pen and a copy of the "Why 2 Rely" handout (p. 15). Then invite half of each group (two to three students) to study the passage and discuss the "hows"—the many ways, according to the psalm, to rely on God. Examples are "Trust in the Lord" and "Be still before the Lord and wait patiently for him." Ask the other half of each team to dig into the "whys"—the reasons, according to the psalm, to rely on God. Examples are "He will make your righteousness shine" and "He will give you the desires of your heart." As the students are busy discussing, encourage them to take notes on their findings.

After a few minutes, have all the students gather and share their hows and whys with one another. Then ask the teams to each evaluate all the reasons they've discussed and to identify their top five answers to the question "Why should we rely on God?"

Bible Application

Commitment Collage

SAY **We've talked about many reasons to rely on God. What has challenged you? Take just a moment to ask yourself this question: "What is the best reason for me to rely on God?"**

While students are thinking, play a CD of reflective Christian music, take the big banner off the wall, and spread it on the floor. Have plenty of markers and crayons available. Invite all of the students to gather around the banner and to write or draw the one reason to rely on God that each has identified.

When students have finished, ask them to form pairs and discuss how they want to rely on God more in their everyday lives. Prompt students to share with each other one specific area of their lives in which they want to grow and to then share one action they'll take in the upcoming week to act on that desire.

In their pairs, have students look up Psalm 46:1 and read the verse aloud. Ask partners to share what the verse means to them in light of what they've just discussed. Invite students to take a few minutes to pray for each other and their commitments to rely on God.

For Extra Impact

Rent *Indiana Jones and the Last Crusade*, and advance the video to one hour, forty-eight minutes, and thirty seconds. Show teenagers the scene in which Indy takes a step of faith on the invisible bridge. Then discuss how it feels to totally rely on God even when such reliance seems to be a huge risk. (For a great resource describing other neat video clips, check out *Group's Blockbuster Movie Illustrations* by Bryan Belknap, Group Publishing, 2001.)

(In general, federal copyright laws do not allow you to use videos—even ones you own—for any purpose other than home viewing. Though some exceptions allow for the use of short segments of copyrighted material for educational purposes, it's best to be on the safe side. Your church can obtain a license from the Motion Picture Licensing Corporation for a small fee. Just visit www.mplc.com or call 1-800-462-8855 for more information.)

In closing, invite the students to return to the banner and write a few words or draw a picture that symbolizes the one way they'll rely on God more. When students have finished working on the banner, ask volunteers to help you tape it to the wall.

SAY **God is more than worthy of our total dependence on him. When we rely on ourselves and our own abilities, we inevitably fail or get off track. God is the one we can turn to who will never let us down. This banner communicates some awesome reasons to trust God as well as some unique ways he's encouraged each of us to rely on him more.**

Close by leading students in this one-sentence prayer based on Psalm 46:1:

SAY **God, you are our refuge and our strength, our ever-present help in trouble. In Jesus' name, amen.**

Faith Journal

Give each student an index card and a pen. Have teenagers write their names and their answers to the following question on their index cards:

• **What is the hardest thing about relying on God?**

After teenagers have written their responses, ask them to return the cards to you. Before you meet with the group again, take time to write personal responses to your students on their index cards. You may want to keep a notebook or a box containing copies of these index cards as well as brief notes of prayer concerns and needs your students share using this assessment tool.

For more information about the Faith Journal option, refer to page 5 of the Introduction.

PSALM 37

How?	Why?
List the many ways David says we should rely on God.	List the many reasons David mentions that we should rely on God.

[think]

research required

Taking It Home

everywhere

take home!

Driving Home the Point:

"August 13, 1944

"Dear Everybody,

"...Does it look like the war will be over soon?

"When it's cold we don't have enough clothing. Send sweaters or something... There is so much bitterness and communism, cynicism, and deep sorrow. The worst for us is not that which we suffer ourselves, but the suffering which we see around us. We also are learning to put the worst in the hands of the Saviour...

"In the morning we walk outside and pray aloud together. Everybody thinks that we are just talking, but then, we *are* just talking—talking with the Saviour, and that is such a joy...

"Keep courage!

"Corrie"

These words were penned by Corrie ten Boom while she was imprisoned in the Nazi concentration camp Vught in Holland. Corrie, her father, and her sister Betsie had been arrested for helping to hide Jews. Her elderly father died after only nine days in a Nazi prison; her sister, who was her best friend, died as well.

Later in her life, Corrie, the author of *The Hiding Place*, wrote about the day they were all arrested, saying, "We did not know what was ahead of us, but I was certain of one thing—that Jesus would never leave us nor forsake us and that, for a child of God, no pit could be so deep that Jesus was not deeper still."

(Corrie ten Boom, *Prison Letters*)

Talking At Home:

As a family, take a trip to the library and find books that contain pictures or information about concentration camps during the Holocaust. Look through them together in order to get a good idea of Corrie ten Boom's living conditions as she wrote her letters. Then discuss these questions:

- **What strikes you about Corrie's attitude? What is so amazing about it?**
- **How do you think Corrie found the strength to maintain that attitude?**

Read Psalm 46:1-3, 10-11.

- **When in your life have the mountains seemed to be falling and the oceans roaring?**
- **How do you usually respond to really difficult situations?**
- **How does it make you feel to know that you can rely on God even in the most difficult moments of your life?**

Corrie's letters from prison and concentration camp are amazing testaments to her faith. As a family, write your own faith letters recounting difficult times in your lives and how God saw you through them. Seal the family's letters in an envelope, and keep them in a special place as a reminder that you can rely on God even in the most difficult times. No pit is so deep that Jesus is not deeper still!

(To find out more about Corrie ten Boom and her family, read *The Hiding Place*.)

Love Is Not Blind; It's Kind!

2 Samuel 9:1-13

2

David Is Merciful to Mephibosheth

 KEY QUESTION: What does it mean to be kind?

 STUDY FOCUS: Students will study David's example of loving others in spite of differences.

KEY VERSE: "Be devoted to one another in brotherly love. Honor one another above yourselves" (ROMANS 12:10).

A Look at the Study

Study Sequence	Minutes	What Students Will Do	Classroom Supplies
Getting Started	5 to 10	**Share and Share Alike?**—Examine the idea of kindness.	Candy
Bible Story Exploration	15 to 20	**How Do I Love Thee?**—Examine David's specific acts of kindness toward Mephibosheth and explore what his other options might have been.	Bibles, paper, pens, overhead projector, transparencies, dry-erase markers
Bible Application	10 to 15	**Read All About It**—Interview one another and report on incidents in which they experienced kindness. Create newspapers containing these interviews.	Newsprint, markers, tape, paper, pens
	10 to 15	**Bury the Hatchet**—Request charity on behalf of an imaginary family. Examine their ability to help people who have offended them in the past.	"Pretty Good Charity" handouts (p. 23), pens
	up to 5	**Faith Journal**—Respond in writing to an aspect of the Key Question.	Index cards, pens

Age-Level Insight

Because peer relationships are so important to teens, group projects are great for generating enthusiasm and participation. However, to prevent the formation of cliques, group membership should change often. Frequent reassigning will help kids acquire the skills they'll need to work with many different kinds of people.

NOTES

After David became king of Israel, he solidified his kingdom. He took Jerusalem from the Jebusites, who had never been driven from the Promised Land. Because of its strategic position on a high ridge near the center of his kingdom, David made Jerusalem his capital city. He set up residence there and named it the City of David.

David also brought the ark of the covenant into Jerusalem. For twenty years it had been kept in a private home, but David moved it to a special tent he had made for it in his kingdom's capital. There he had sacrifices made to God and blessed the people of Israel. Then David himself prayed before the Lord, acknowledging God's greatness and mercy and asking for God's blessing on the kingdom of Israel (2 Samuel 7:18-29).

David's forces continued to conquer surrounding nations so that Israel was no longer oppressed by people who had not been driven out when the Hebrews first entered the Promised Land. He became famous for his military prowess, and God gave him victory wherever he went (2 Samuel 8:13-14). And we are told that David did "what was just and right for all his people" (2 Samuel 8:15).

It is against this backdrop that the story of Mephibosheth unfolded. David was secure in his position, and he had practiced doing what was right. Now he had time to remember his old friend Jonathan, and he wanted to help Jonathan's descendants. Most kings of that time would have sought out any descendants of the former king and executed them so that they would never be a threat to the throne. But that was not David's concern. Instead he wanted to honor the friend who had saved his life.

When he was a child, Mephibosheth was crippled when he fell while fleeing with his nurse after Jonathan and Saul had been killed in battle (2 Samuel 4:4). Now he was likely in hiding, fearing that David would harm him. When summoned to the king, Mephibosheth bowed before David, possibly fearing for his life. Instead David offered kindness and honor. Not only did David give Mephibosheth all the land that had belonged to Saul and his family, but he also gave Mephibosheth a seat of honor at the king's own table, as if Mephibosheth were David's own son.

David's kindness to Mephibosheth went far beyond the cultural expectations of the time. It demonstrated David's integrity and showed how important it was to him to show love and mercy.

Getting Started

Share and Share Alike?

Greet students and tell them you need some help with a few chores before class begins. Assign tasks such as sweeping the floor, shelving books, sharpening pencils, and emptying trash cans. When you've assigned a few chores to only a few students, pretend you've reached the end of your list. Then wait to see if the students who didn't get an assignment offer to help the ones who did. Afterward, as a "reward," distribute candy to all but a few students (whether or not they helped with the cleaning chores), then pretend to have run out of candy. See if anyone offers to share or give up his or her candy. After kids have had a chance to share, distribute candy to anyone who didn't get any earlier.

SAY **I was curious to see how you would handle these situations. I purposely arranged it so that some of you ended up with chores or candy and some of you didn't. I hope this exercise helped you begin thinking about kindness.**

ASK • **What are some specific ways in which people show kindness?**
• **What demonstrations of kindness have we seen in class today?**
• **Do you think kindness matters to God? Explain.**
• **What does it mean to be kind?**

Bible Story Exploration

How Do I Love Thee?

Read aloud 2 Samuel 9:1-13.

Have students form groups of three, and give each trio a transparency and one dry-erase marker.

SAY **Now I want you to pretend you are a TV sports commentator. Using the transparencies and markers I've supplied, I want each group to draw a diagram using arrows and symbols to show who did what in 2 Samuel 9:1-13.**

If necessary, describe how sports commentators draw diagrams during football games to explain which key players went where, and why. To help students get started, suggest that trios first come up with a list of facts (that is, who did what). Tell students they may label their symbols if they choose. Finally, have kids circle all gestures of kindness.

When all the groups have finished, ask a volunteer to place his or her group's diagram on the overhead projector and explain the diagram to everyone.

SAY **David returned Mephibosheth's family's land to him, he gave**

Last Week's Impact

As teenagers arrive, greet them warmly, and ask follow-up questions to review last week's study and Key Verse. Ask questions such as "How did you rely on God last week?" and "Why did you rely on God?"

If you used the Faith Journal option last week, take this time to return your students' index cards to them.

for OLDER teenagers

Instead of asking students to help with chores in the classroom, have them pass around a sign-up sheet for volunteers to help with projects on the church grounds at a later date. List jobs such as mowing the lawn, weeding a garden, washing windows, and doing the dishes after a special function. Make sure there are fewer chores on the list than students (but plenty of room for everyone to sign up for jobs others have signed up for), and collect the list when all the chores have been claimed.

him the services of Ziba and Ziba's household, and he invited Mephibosheth to dine at his table. In biblical times, sitting down together for a meal was considered an intimate act. The table was a place to cultivate important relationships. In effect, David made Mephibosheth an honored member of his family by reserving a permanent place for him at his table.

Distribute paper and pens, and ask each trio to list the three acts of kindness that David performed for Mephibosheth. Then ask them to think of five other acts of kindness David could have done for Mephibosheth.

What acts of Kindness could [handwritten margin note]

SAY After you've thought of five more acts of kindness, I want you to rank the eight kind gestures listed on your paper, with the first one being the kindest one you think David could have made.

ASK • What kinds of things have people always wanted from one another? from life?
• Which gifts of kindness on your list are tangible (that is, capable of being touched), and which ones are intangible?

SAY Romans 12:10 provides two clues about what it means to be kind.

Ask a volunteer to read the verse aloud.

ASK • According to the author of this verse, what are two ways to show kindness?

SAY Let's talk about kindness we've experienced in our lives.

Bible Application

Read All About It

Distribute paper and pens as students form pairs. Ask partners to interview each other by asking the following question. (Tell them to be sure to take notes as their partners respond.)

ASK • What's the kindest thing anyone has ever done for you?

After students have conducted their interviews, give them more paper, and ask each student to write a brief newspaper article describing the incident that was related in the interview. Remind teenagers to supply the facts (who, what, where, and when). Then have each pair join another pair to form a group of four. Give each foursome markers and a sheet of newsprint. Tell groups to illustrate their stories and write headlines for them. Have foursomes tape their stories to the newsprint, name their newspapers, and fold them any way they choose.

Encourage volunteers to share their creations with the entire group.

SAY Based on what we've heard and read here today, it appears that people's words and actions are as important to us as they were to people in King David's time. We all want to be on the receiving end of kindness, but God wants us to dish it out, too.

Bury the Hatchet

SAY Now I want you to rejoin your trio and imagine that the other two members of your trio are your immediate family. It's the Christmas season, and your family has decided to "adopt" a needy family. A local charitable organization will supervise the project to help ensure that your adopted family has a good Christmas.

However, there's one catch: The family you've been assigned lives in your neighborhood, and it isn't exactly one of your family's favorites. For starters, they've ignored your mom's requests to prevent their dog from coming into your yard and picking fights with your dog. Besides that, they frequently hold loud parties that keep you up long into the night. Also, one of the daughters, who rides your school bus, was whispering and giggling with her friend while looking at you one day. But the fact remains that the father has just lost his job, and there are four kids in the family.

Give each trio a copy of the "Pretty Good Charity" handout (p. 23), and tell each trio to write a proposal for submission to the Pretty Good Charity board of directors. The proposal should describe the specific things the family will do for the adopted family. After ten minutes, have a volunteer from each trio present the trio's proposal.

ASK • Were any of the plans you created similar to the kindness David showed Mephibosheth? Explain.
• Was it hard to set aside your negative feelings in order to campaign for your adopted family? Explain.
• How can we get past negative feelings and be kind toward people who have hurt us?
• Why should we be kind toward people who have hurt us?
• How is God's mercy toward us similar to David's mercy toward Mephibosheth?

Have students each tell the other members of their trios the name of one person they would like to show kindness to in the upcoming week. After students have shared, ask them to pray that the members of their trios will remain committed to share God's kindness with others.

SAY Today you've learned how powerful kindness can be. You have a great opportunity to show God's kindness to others this week. Watch for those opportunities, and pray for God's help in taking advantage of them.

Close the meeting with a short prayer for your students as they attempt to show kindness to others.

For Extra Impact

Supply a tape recorder, camera, or camcorder for students' use as they conduct their interviews. Make a computer and printer available so that students may type and arrange their articles. If teenagers enjoy this activity, challenge them to write and submit true stories about promises kept and kindnesses extended. Use these stories to create a Good News Gazette. Post the newspaper where church members can read it, or "deliver" the paper to people attending an upcoming church service. You might even sell the Gazette as a fund-raising effort!

Faith Journal

Give each student an index card and a pen. Have teenagers write their names and their answers to the following question on their index cards:

• **How does God help you to be kind?**

After teenagers have written their responses, ask them to return the cards to you. Before you meet with the group again, take time to write personal responses to your students on their index cards. You may want to keep a notebook or a box containing copies of these index cards as well as brief notes of prayer concerns and needs your students share using this assessment tool.

For more information about the Faith Journal option, refer to page 5 of the Introduction.

Pretty Good Charity

Use the space below to write a proposal to submit to the Pretty Good Charity board of directors. Outline specific things you'd like to do on behalf of your adopted family.

_____

_____

_____

_____

_____

_____

_____

_____

_____

_____

_____

_____

_____

_____

_____

_____

_____

_____

_____

_____

[think]

research required

take home! everywhere

Talking About It

Driving Home the Point:

"No act of kindness, no matter how small, is ever wasted."

(Aesop, "The Lion and the Mouse")

Talking At **Home:**

With your family, read Luke 10:25-37, the parable of the good Samaritan. In this parable, Jesus says the true neighbor was the person who was merciful to the man in need. Ironically enough, in this case, the merciful person was someone whom Jews in Jesus' time regarded as inferior for political and cultural reasons. Discuss the following questions with your family:

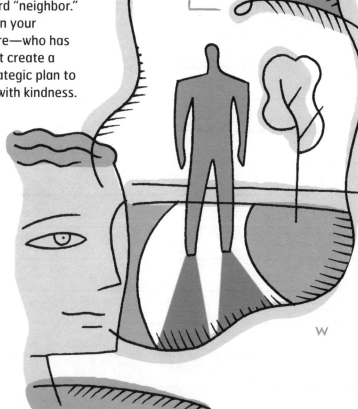

- **What does it mean to be kind?**
- **What sometimes makes it hard to be merciful?**
- **Why does God want us to be merciful?**
- **In what ways has God shown us mercy?**

As a family, define the word "neighbor." Then identify someone—in your neighborhood or elsewhere—who has offended your family. Next create a "kindness contract," a strategic plan to replace your resentment with kindness. Agree on specific steps you are willing to take, and establish deadlines for taking them. Have everyone sign and date the contract.

What Should We Do When We Sin?

2 Samuel 11:1–12:10;
Psalm 51:1-12

3

Nathan Confronts David About His Sin

 KEY QUESTION: What should we do when we sin?

 STUDY FOCUS: Students will realize that we all make mistakes that make us less than God wants us to be and that only when we acknowledge our wrongdoing can we draw closer to him.

KEY VERSE: "If we confess our sins, he is faithful and just and will forgive us our sins and purify us from all unrighteousness" (1 John 1:9).

A Look at the Study

Study Sequence	Minutes	What Students Will Do	Classroom Supplies
Getting Started	up to 10	**Sticky Situation**—Spin a "spider web," try to escape from it, and talk about the consequences of deceit.	Newsprint, marker, tape, yarn
Bible Story Exploration	up to 10	**Splish Splash (She Was Taking a Bath)**—Examine David's behavior toward Bathsheba and Uriah and participate in a mock trial.	Newsprint, marker, Bibles
	up to 10	**Busted! David Faces His Sin**—Examine the specifics and consequences of David's sin.	Newsprint, marker, Bibles, paper, pens
Bible Application	up to 10	**Mirror, Mirror on the Wall**—Discuss the experience of being confronted about a sin and explore the idea of repentance.	Newsprint, marker, Bible
	15 to 20	**I Beg Your Pardon**—Speculate about God's reactions to apologies.	Bowl, paper, pens
	up to 5	**Faith Journal**—Respond in writing to an aspect of the Key Question.	Index cards, pens

Age-Level Insight

Depending on their level of maturity, individual teens may find it difficult to talk about the sexual relationship between David and Bathsheba. Expect some teens to be embarrassed into silence and others to pretend to have more experience than they actually possess. To facilitate discussions and keep them on track, you might want to circulate among discussion groups and "drop in" on their conversations. It's natural to feel awkward talking about sex, but everyone will be more comfortable if you stick to the facts of the story and acknowledge that sexual temptations are common and powerful and that giving in to them always has consequences.

NOTES

The events in this story probably occurred about ten years after David had established himself as king in Jerusalem, so he would have been forty-seven years old at the time. Although his soldiers went out to battle, it wasn't necessary or wise for David to risk his life to do so. Instead he directed the fighting through messengers sent back and forth between him and Joab, his general.

David didn't maintain a large year-round army. At that time, the world was largely agrarian, and farmers had to mind their crops at certain times of the year. So after the grain harvest in April and May, the farmer-soldiers were able to fight with the army, making the spring, especially late spring, a convenient time for war.

David's walk on the roof was not unusual. Roofs at that time and in that place were flat, and David had probably gone up to the roof to relax in the evening air. Bathsheba was likely bathing herself as part of the purification ritual required after menstruation. She may not have realized she could be seen from the palace roof; however, some have suggested that she knew she could be seen and may have been hoping that the king would notice her.

The comment in 2 Samuel 11:4 that Bathsheba had just purified herself from her "uncleanness" (menstruation) establishes that she was not made pregnant by her husband, Uriah, because he was away fighting in the war.

In summoning Uriah home from the war, David hoped that Uriah would sleep with Bathsheba so that later, when the baby was born, no one would suspect that the baby wasn't Uriah's. It may seem odd that Uriah steadfastly refused to sleep with his wife, but in fact it was not unusual for Israelite soldiers to take a vow of sexual abstinence during times of war. They felt it was wrong to indulge their own pleasures while their fellow soldiers were fighting.

Although Nathan was a prophet, it took tremendous courage for him to confront David about his sin. Remember that David had already killed once to cover up his sin with Bathsheba. What was to stop him from killing again to cover up the sin of killing Uriah? In spite of that possibility, Nathan did what God sent him to do.

Nathan's prophecy came true: David and Bathsheba's firstborn son died, David's son Absalom incited a rebellion against him in which David was driven from Jerusalem, and Absalom slept with David's concubines.

David eloquently proclaims his remorse and repentance in Psalm 51. David's sin devastated him and his kingdom, but he sought forgiveness in one of the most beautiful psalms of contrition ever written. His plea for cleansing is an example for us all, who, like David, are sinners.

Getting Started

Sticky Situation

Before students arrive, write the following quotation and questions on a sheet of newsprint, and post the newsprint where everyone can see it:

"Oh, what a tangled web we weave, when first we practice to deceive!" (Sir Walter Scott)

- How did it feel to crawl out of the web you created?

- Can you think of a time you or someone you know got into a tangled mess by being deceitful? Explain.

- Who was fooled and perhaps hurt by the deceit?

- How did the incident make you feel?

- What should you do when you deceive others?

Ask students to stand in the center of the room and face outward. Place six or seven chairs in a circle around the students, then give one student a skein of yarn. Direct students to start spinning a "spider web" around the group, using the chairs to anchor the yarn and to give the web a framework. When students reach the end of the skein, have them wait until you give the signal for them to crawl through the web they've just created. Challenge them to go *through* the web (without breaking it!) rather than ducking under or climbing over it.

Have students form pairs and discuss the quotation and questions you posted earlier.

Bible Story Exploration

Splish Splash (She Was Taking a Bath)

SAY Today we're going to talk about the temptation to be deceitful and God's response to deceit. Specifically, we're going to see how King David, a man after God's heart, made a terrible mistake and then made it worse by trying to cover it up.

Form three groups: the prosecuting attorneys, the defense attorneys, and the jury. Instruct everyone to read 2 Samuel 11:1-27, and then ask the class to help you "bring charges" against King David for his behavior. As kids verbalize David's offenses, list them on a sheet of newsprint. Then give attorneys time to formulate their arguments against or in defense of David. After each group of attorneys has presented its arguments, give the jury a few minutes to agree on a verdict and, if applicable, a penalty.

Last Week's Impact

As teenagers arrive, greet them warmly, and ask follow-up questions to review last week's lesson and Key Verse. Ask questions such as "What does kindness mean to you?" and "How did you show kindness during the past week?"

If you used the Faith Journal option last week, take this time to return your students' index cards to them.

Tip From the Trenches

Have a dictionary or thesaurus handy to expand upon students' understanding of the word "deceit."

Tip From the Trenches

This activity will work best if you tell students to weave their web from the floor to at least waist height.

For Extra Impact

Read aloud from *The Cat in the Hat Comes Back* by Dr. Seuss. Use this classic children's story to jump-start a discussion about our feeble attempts at "damage control" and how we sometimes try to hide our messes rather than owning up to them. Talk about the role of human pride and our tendency to make things worse when we attempt to cover up our mistakes.

Busted! David Faces His Sin

Write each of the following sets of questions on a separate sheet of newsprint, and post the newsprint in three corners of the room. Number each of the students in your class from one to three. Have all the "ones" go to one corner of the room, all the "twos" go to another corner, and all the "threes" go to yet another corner. Tell students they're all responsible for reading 2 Samuel 12:1-10 and Psalm 51:1-12 and discussing the questions posted in their corners. Ask all the students to jot their groups' answers on a sheet of paper.

Ones:

- Why do you think God objects to adultery?

- Besides committing adultery, how did David sin?

- What adjectives would you use to describe David's sinful actions?

Twos:

- Why do you think God sent Nathan to point out David's sin?

- How do you interpret Nathan's parable?

- Do you think the punishment God promised was appropriate to David's crime? Explain.

Threes:

- How would you describe David's attitude in Psalm 51?

- What, besides forgiveness, did David ask for in this psalm?

- What are some signs that a person is genuinely sorry to have sinned?

After the students have met in their assigned corners and discussed their answers to the questions posted there, have them return to the center of the room and report what they've learned.

SAY **It's interesting that David eventually went very public with his sin; he even wrote a song about it. He tried to hide it initially, but ultimately he confessed it to everyone who had ears to hear.**

I'd like you to find a partner and talk about a time someone confronted you—or you confronted someone—about a sin or wrongdoing.

Bible Application

Mirror, Mirror on the Wall

As pairs are discussing their personal experiences, write the following questions on another sheet of newsprint:

- What was the immediate reaction of the person who was confronted about the wrongdoing?

- Do you agree or disagree that "love means never having to say you're sorry"? Explain.
- Do you think it's fair to punish someone who has repented? Explain.

After students have shared their stories with their partners, give each pair several minutes to discuss the questions written on the newsprint.

Read 1 John 1:9 aloud.

ASK
- **What excuses do people sometimes use to justify their wrongdoing?**
- **What should we do when we sin?**
- **What elements should a confession or repentance contain?**
- **What is good about remorse or shame?**

I Beg Your Pardon

Distribute paper and pens. Form four groups, and explain that you'd like each group to write a confession from the perspective of someone who's been caught doing something wrong. First each group will create its own scenario in which the wrongdoing is discovered then write a confession. Have one group write a reluctant, halfhearted apology; have the second group make light of the wrongdoing; have the third group dance around the accusation altogether, never quite apologizing; and have the fourth group write a sincere apology. Finally, ask a volunteer from each group to read the guilty person's confession to the entire class. Have students jot down their personal reactions to each of these confessions.

ASK
- **What was your reaction to each of these apologies?**
- **How do you think God would react to each of these apologies?**
- **What should we do when we sin?**

SAY David thought he could cleverly disguise his sin, but he soon learned that God was well aware of it. God punished David but also accepted David's apology and continued to bless David in many ways. Even though God holds us accountable for our sins, he accepts our sincere repentance.

Now I'd like you to think about a time you did something wrong, preferably something you haven't admitted before. I want you to write an apology for it, as though you were writing a note to God. (For the purposes of this activity, you don't have to reveal your identity.) Then fold up your note, and hold it up when you're ready for me to collect it.

When teenagers have finished writing, have them drop their confessions into a bowl or another container. Offer a prayer of confession to God after you've collected all the notes .

Faith Journal

Give each student an index card and a pen. Have teenagers write their

Tip From the Trenches

Be sure to dispose of the notes before any of your curious students have had a chance to look through them.

Tip From the Trenches

To help strengthen the connection between church and home, photocopy the "Taking It Home" page at the end of this study, and either distribute copies to students before they leave or mail them to their homes. Encourage students to complete the reading, activities, and discussion with their families during the coming week.

names and their answers to the following question on their index cards:

- **How does confession affect our relationships with God and others?**

After teenagers have written their responses, ask them to return the cards to you. Before you meet with the group again, take time to write personal responses to your students on their index cards. You may want to keep a notebook or a box containing copies of these index cards as well as brief notes of prayer concerns and needs your students share using this assessment tool.

For more information about the Faith Journal option, refer to page 5 of the Introduction.

Talking About It

Driving Home the Point:

> At last [David] had confessed his sin, and now he found himself in deep spiritual hunger and desiring to be reconciled with God."
>
> (Walter C. Kaiser Jr. et al, *Hard Sayings of the Bible*)

Talking At Home:

As a family, take turns talking about a time each of you made a mess of something. (It's OK if young kids talk about having made a literal mess.) Find a piece of silver that's badly tarnished, a piece of old furniture that's quite dusty, or something like a hurricane lamp that has soot on it. Use polish or cleaner to restore the item to its former luster, then read Jeremiah 15:19 aloud. Discuss these questions:

- How are we like the item we just cleaned up?
- What does God want us to do about the messes we make?
- What does God mean when he says he will "restore" us?
- After we've been restored, what does God expect us to do?

The Selfish Path to Destruction

2 Samuel 15:1-12;
17:1-12; 18:1-8

4

Absalom Rebels and Is Defeated

 KEY QUESTION: Why is a self-centered attitude wrong?

 STUDY FOCUS: Students will be prompted to think about the difference between "self-hood" and servanthood.

KEY VERSE: "He has showed you, O man, what is good. And what does the Lord require of you? To act justly and to love mercy and to walk humbly with your God" (MICAH 6:8).

A Look at the Study

Study Sequence	Minutes	What Students Will Do	Classroom Supplies
Getting Started	15 to 20	**Survivor**—Form teams and compete to see which team is strongest.	Water pitchers, glasses, toilet paper, Bibles, masking tape
Bible Story Exploration	5 to 10	**Absalom Builds a Power Base**—Write news reports about the growth of Absalom's "corporate stock."	Bibles, bell, confetti, pens, paper
	10 to 15	**The Antitrust Breakup**—Write news reports about Absalom's defeat.	Bibles, paper, pens
Bible Application	15 to 20	**Growing a Servant Attitude**—Identify three ways they need to change in order to have a servant attitude.	Bibles, slips of paper, pens
	up to 5	**Faith Journal**—Respond in writing to an aspect of the Key Question.	Index cards, pens

Age-Level Insight

Teenagers strive so hard to be accepted by their peers that they often focus on themselves and their personal success instead of a servant attitude. They worry whether it will be cool to help the underdog or to hang with the less popular. God's promise is that success comes through the denial of self rather than the exaltation of self. Help your kids understand that human popularity, wealth, and acceptance are temporal matters but that following the will of God is an eternal pursuit.

NOTES

The son born from David and Bathsheba's sin died, even though David pleaded with God to spare him. Soon Bathsheba bore David a second son, Solomon.

It's important to know about certain events in the lives of David's other children in order to understand the context in which today's story took place. Amnon, one of David's sons, was attracted to Tamar, a daughter of David and half-sister to Amnon. He was so obsessed with her that he pretended to be sick and deceived her into coming to his bedroom to take care of him. When she did, he raped her. But after the rape, Amnon suddenly turned against her and kicked her out. Absalom, Tamar's brother and another of David's sons, took her in. Both David and Absalom were furious, but David, the king and father who could have punished Amnon, did nothing. Two years later, Absalom had Amnon murdered and then fled from David and Israel. David mourned for Amnon and wished to be reunited with Absalom (2 Samuel 13:37-39).

After Absalom had been gone three years, Joab, David's trusted general, had seen enough of David's pain. He enlisted a "wise woman" to confront David and convince him to allow Absalom to return to Israel. David agreed, but apparently he was hesitant to fully forgive and restore Absalom, because he refused to see him after his return. It took setting Joab's field on fire two years later for Absalom to finally get the king's attention and be allowed to visit his father. Absalom bowed to the ground before David, and David kissed him, offering forgiveness.

After that meeting, Absalom put a subversive plan into action. He would meet people coming into Jerusalem, criticize his father's system of administering justice, and promise a better one if he were made king. He treated the people as equals, not as if they were below him, as indicated in his response to those who bowed before him (2 Samuel 15:5-6). In this way, he won over large numbers of people.

When he was about thirty years old, Absalom decided to revolt openly, and he chose Hebron for his headquarters. David had been proclaimed king in Hebron, and Absalom had been born there; it was a significant place of worship; it was the city David had abandoned when he moved his capital to Jerusalem. Absalom must have counted all these factors in his favor.

David must have realized that Absalom had gained quite a following, because when he heard of the revolt, he insisted on fleeing Jerusalem for safety. After receiving conflicting advice, Absalom decided not to attack David right away. The delay allowed David time to muster an army (2 Samuel 18:1). In the ensuing battle, twenty thousand died. In the end, Absalom was killed by Joab, and David again wept over the death of a son. Self-centered attitudes and actions had taken the life of yet another of the king's sons.

Getting Started

Survivor

Begin by telling students that today's study is about having a servant attitude. Form teams of no more than ten students each. Explain that each team will choose a different person to participate in each of the events described below. Participants who lose a particular event for their teams will be eliminated from the competition and must sit down. Before beginning the first round, emphasize the fact that students must work as a team in order to win. Here are the events:

- Event 1: Give each team a pitcher of water and a glass. One member of each team will drink until all the water in the pitcher is gone. The fastest drinker is the winner of the event.

- Event 2: Give each team a roll of toilet paper. The goal is to totally wrap one team member in the paper. Each team must use an entire roll. The first person to be mummified is the winner of the event.

- Event 3: Give each team a Bible. One member of each team will read Psalm 100 aloud. The first person to finish reading the psalm is the winner of the event.

- Event 4: Use masking tape to mark a starting line and a finish line on the floor. One member of each team will hop to the finish line. The fastest hopper is the winner of the event.

- Event 5: One member of each team will sing "The Star-Spangled Banner" followed by "Silent Night" and "Three Blind Mice." The first person to complete all three songs is the winner of the event.

After a winner has been declared in each of the five events, ask losing teams to appoint new representatives to participate in a second round. Continue in this manner until only one person remains. You may have to hold three or four rounds, depending on the size of your group. When there are fewer than five members on a team, someone on that team will have to participate in more than one event, until finally one person must compete in all the events. The winning team is the one with the last person to survive all the events.

ASK
- **Why was it more difficult to be successful as the team got smaller?**
- **Do you prefer to compete alone or in a team?**
- **How does a person with an individualistic attitude affect a team?**
- **Why is a self-centered attitude wrong?**

SAY **To find the answer to that question, let's examine what happens when people strive for success at the expense of others.**

Last Week's Impact

As teenagers arrive, greet them warmly, and ask follow-up questions to review last week's study and Key Verse. Ask questions such as "What does confession mean to you?" and "How does it feel to be forgiven?"

If you used the Faith Journal option last week, take this time to return your students' index cards to them.

Teacher SkillBuilder

We all learn by example. If we exemplify the attitudes we would like to teach our students, they will begin to mirror our behavior. Ask yourself this week, "What does a servant attitude look like? Is it possible to climb the corporate ladder and at the same time model Christlike service? What impact do bouts of anger have on my ability to model an others-oriented attitude?" Students do not accept our words at face value, and neither does God. Make sure you practice what you preach this week.

Bible Story Exploration

Absalom Builds a Power Base

Ask students to remain in their teams from the previous activity and to read 2 Samuel 15:1-12 with the idea of writing a news story about how Absalom gained his power. Distribute paper and a pen to each group, then have each team develop a news report about the growing strength of a company called Absalom Enterprises. When students have finished, ask each team to deliver its newscast, complete with the sound of a bell signaling the opening of the stock exchange and confetti to simulate ticker tape.

The Antitrust Breakup

Have students remain in their groups and read 2 Samuel 17:1-12 and 18:1-8 together. Then have each group write the second part of its report on Absalom Enterprises, focusing this time on the company's downfall. Have each group present its news report.

ASK • **Why was Absalom's approach to rapid growth not the best method he could have used?**

SAY **All things prosperous are not necessarily good; spending time growing "things" is selfish and not what God desires of those who follow him.**

Bible Application

Growing a Servant Attitude

Have students open their Bibles to the book of Micah, and read Micah 6:8 aloud.

Give everyone three slips of paper, and ask students to label each slip "Attitude Adjustment."

SAY **I'd like you to take a few moments to prayerfully reflect on one way that you can live the Micah passage at home, one way you can live it at school, and one way you can live it with friends. Then I would like you to write on each slip your name and one way you need to change in order to become less self-centered and more God-centered. Please write something different on each slip.**

When students have finished, ask them to form a circle and sit down.

SAY **Now I would like you to place your three Attitude Adjustments in the center of the circle as a symbol of your commitment to change.**

ASK
• **Was it difficult for you to identify three areas in your life that should be changed?**
• **In what kind of situations is it most difficult to adopt a servant's attitude?**
• **How can you be more in tune with God's will for your life and your actions?**

Have everyone find a partner and share the three Attitude Adjustments he or she has identified. Then say a prayer asking God to help your students adjust their attitudes to be more like God's.

End the study by having students reclaim the Attitude Adjustments of their partners so that they may use them as reminders to pray for their partners during the upcoming week.

Faith Journal

Give each student an index card and a pen. Have teenagers write their names and their answers to the following question on their index cards:

• **How can you be less self-centered and more God-centered?**

After teenagers have written their responses, ask them to return the cards to you. Before you meet with the group again, take time to write personal responses to your students on their index cards. You may want to keep a notebook or a box containing copies of these index cards as well as brief notes of prayer concerns and needs your students share using this assessment tool.

For more information about the Faith Journal option, refer to page 5 of the Introduction.

Tip From
the **Trenches**

To help strengthen the connection between church and home, photocopy the "Taking It Home" page at the end of this study, and either distribute copies to students before they leave or mail them to their homes. Encourage students to complete the reading, activities, and discussion with their families during the coming week.

Driving Home the Point:

"Treat everyone with kindness and equal respect; you never know whom you're talking to."

(Kevin Freiberg and Jackie Freiberg, *Nuts! Southwest Airlines' Crazy Recipe for Business and Personal Success*)

Talking At Home:

Read Micah 6:8 with your family, and discuss these questions:

- **Do you sometimes find it difficult to focus on the needs and desires of others in the family instead of your own? Explain.**
- **Why is it important to understand what God desires of us in our relationships?**

Read Philippians 2:5-11 together, and identify ways that your family can emulate Jesus' servant attitude. Work with your family to create a family mission statement that focuses on the importance of nurturing an attitude of service without sacrificing each family member's individuality.

A Real Wiseguy

1 Kings 2:1-4; 3:3-28

5

Solomon Rules Wisely

 KEY QUESTION: How can we get wisdom?

 STUDY FOCUS: Students will be challenged to understand the difference between "human smarts" and "Christlike wisdom."

KEY VERSE: "If any of you lacks wisdom, he should ask God, who gives generously to all without finding fault, and it will be given to him" (James 1:5).

A Look at the Study

Study Sequence	Minutes	What Students Will Do	Classroom Supplies
Getting Started	15 to 20	**Wisdom Test**—Complete a wisdom survey.	"Wisdom Test" handouts (p. 43), pens
Bible Story Exploration	5 to 10	**Solomon's Wisdom**—Explore the life of Solomon and decide if he was wise or just intelligent.	Bibles
	10 to 15	**Wisdom Scriptures**—Research the Bible to find various passages related to wisdom.	Bibles, poster board, markers, tape
Bible Application	15 to 20	**Hidden Treasures**—Illustrate how diligently we search for earthly answers instead of scriptural ones.	Coins in various denominations
	up to 5	**Faith Journal**—Respond in writing to an aspect of the Key Question.	Index cards, pens

Age-Level Insight

 Teenagers may find it difficult to distinguish between wisdom and intelligence. They have spent many years in school increasing their human knowledge, but they may have spent very little time developing Christlike wisdom. Use this study to help students understand that God will always provide wise choices to life's tough decisions if they will turn to him instead of counting solely on their own decision-making processes.

NOTES

After Absalom's revolt, David again won the hearts of the people (2 Samuel 19:14). Despite other opposition that arose from time to time, David continued to reign successfully for many years. But when David was old and near death, one of his sons, Adonijah, turned against David's wishes and set himself up as king. But David had Solomon, his second son with Bathsheba, anointed as king by Nathan the prophet and Zadok the priest. Adonijah quickly realized that Solomon was favored by the people and sought refuge from Solomon. Solomon gave him a second chance and allowed him to go home, promising not to kill him if he proved himself loyal.

David's charge to Solomon in 1 Kings 2:2-4 echoes the words of Deuteronomy 11. Apart from his sin with Bathsheba, David had consistently been obedient to God throughout his life, and he advised his son to do the same. God had promised David that his descendants would remain on the throne as long as they honored God. David's wish was for Solomon as well as for himself.

Once established on the throne, Solomon sought to follow the Lord. His habit of offering sacrifices at the "high places" (1 Kings 3:3) was questionable, however. The high places were altars left from the pagan worship prevalent in Canaan before the Israelites took over the land. Even though the law of Moses demanded that the Israelites not use pagan altars for worshipping God, it appears that this was a common practice in Solomon's time. After all, there was not yet a temple at which to worship. Gibeon was an important place of worship because the tabernacle and the bronze altar were kept there (1 Chronicles 21:29; 2 Chronicles 1:2-6). God must have honored Solomon's worship and sacrifices there to some degree because God appeared to Solomon there and offered Solomon whatever he wanted.

Solomon's request for wisdom pleased God. Solomon could have asked for power, riches, or fame; instead he unselfishly asked for what would help him best rule God's people. God honored Solomon's unselfishness by granting his wish and giving him power, riches, and fame as well. Solomon's response was to return to Jerusalem and again offer sacrifices to God.

The best-known example of Solomon's wisdom is related in 1 Kings 3:16-28. This story dramatically illustrates the creative wisdom God bestowed upon Solomon. The final verse of this passage relates the people's wonder when they witnessed their king's wisdom. Solomon had asked God for discernment in ruling God's people, and there was no doubt that his prayer was answered.

Getting Started

Wisdom Test

Begin by telling students that the subject of today's study is true wisdom.

Give each student a pen and a "Wisdom Test" handout (p. 43). Allow everyone five minutes to answer the questions, then ask your students to form pairs to discuss their answers.

ASK • **Why do we sometimes feel as if we lack wisdom in certain areas of our lives?**
• **How can we get wisdom?**

SAY **God desires to give us wisdom if we ask for it. Today we're going to study a person in the Bible who desired wisdom, asked God for it, and became what some consider to be the wisest man in the world!**

Bible Story Exploration

Solomon's Wisdom

Have students form pairs. Ask each pair to read the story of Solomon in 1 Kings 2:1-4; 3:3-28. Then ask each pair to rate Solomon's wisdom on a scale of one to ten, one being smart and ten being wise. Once the pairs have rated Solomon, have them line up on an imaginary line based on their ratings. Have pairs share with the group the rationale for their decisions.

ASK • **What are some of the standards by which we rate wisdom?**
• **When we ask God for wisdom, do you think he will always give it to us? Why or why not?**
• **How can we get wisdom from God?**

SAY **God desires to make us as wise as Solomon. He also desires that we play a role in the process of gaining wisdom. Let's explore how we can seek wisdom from God through his Word.**

Wisdom Scriptures

Form five teams (or, if your group is small, have students do this activity individually or in pairs). Give each team poster board and markers. Assign one of the following Scriptures to each team. Have each team read its assigned Scripture and then illustrate on the poster board the wisdom principle conveyed in the Scripture. When students have completed this part of the activity, post the illustrations on the wall to show a scriptural view of wisdom.

• Psalm 119:97-104

• Proverbs 11:2

• Proverbs 29:15

Last Week's Impact

As teenagers arrive, greet them warmly, and ask follow-up questions to review last week's study and Key Verse. Ask questions such as "How can we honor God with our attitudes?" and "What does a servant attitude look like?"

If you used the Faith Journal option last week, take this time to return your students' index cards to them.

For Extra Impact

You may make the "Wisdom Test" more interactive by asking the first question aloud and having everyone who responds "a" go to one corner of the room, the "b's" to a different spot, and so on. This will allow students to see how many people feel as they do. Then have volunteers from all the groups explain why they chose their answers.

for Younger teenagers

Instead of asking younger students to write wisdom principles on poster board, have students act them out as the others guess which wisdom principles they are depicting.

Finally, ask the group to read the Key Verse, James 1:5, aloud and to illustrate the passage together.

ASK • **Based on all of these passages, how do you think a person gets wisdom?**
• **Why would someone choose not to seek God's wisdom?**

SAY **God desires to give you all the wisdom you need. He wants to give each of us the wisdom of Solomon. Let's find out how we can get it.**

Bible Application

Hidden Treasures

Before class, hide various denominations of coins around the room. (Real money works best, but play money will convey the same point.) Tell students that you have hidden treasures around the classroom and that whoever finds them may keep them. (Of course, the higher the denomination, the harder students will search!) When all the money is found, bring students together and discuss how diligently they searched for the treasure. Have the students form groups of four and discuss the following questions.

ASK • **How determined were you to find the cash?**
• **What process did you use in your search?**
• **How is this similar to seeking God's wisdom?**
• **Do you plan to begin a diligent search for God's wisdom this week? If so, how do you plan to do it?**
• **What earthly treasures often stand in the way of finding godly direction?**

Have students form pairs and pray for each other, asking God to give them wisdom in dealing with obstacles to finding God's direction. Have partners commit to praying for each other during the upcoming week.

Faith Journal

Give each student an index card and a pen. Have teenagers write their names and their answers to the following question on their index cards:

• **How can you diligently seek God's wisdom?**

After teenagers have written their responses, ask them to return the cards to you. Before you meet with the group again, take time to write personal responses to your students on their index cards. You may want to keep a notebook or a box containing copies of these index cards as well as brief notes of prayer concerns and needs your students share using this assessment tool.

For more information about the Faith Journal option, refer to page 5 of the Introduction.

Teacher SkillBuilder

Wisdom is a concept that often eludes adults as well as teenagers. Instead of turning to God, we rely on our own abilities to solve problems. If we begin to understand scriptural wisdom as portrayed in the book of Proverbs, we will begin to understand an all-knowing God who desires to share his knowledge, power, and wisdom with powerless, foolish creatures like us. Tell teenagers about times you made your own decisions without consulting God, and talk about how those decisions affected your life. Also share instances in which you trusted in God's wisdom and were able to see the wonderful benefits of relying on him.

Tip From the Trenches

To help strengthen the connection between church and home, photocopy the "Taking It Home" page at the end of this study, and either distribute copies to students before they leave or mail them to their homes. Encourage students to complete the reading, activities, and discussion with their families during the coming week.

Wisdom Test

I. *My friends think of me as...*

❑ a. foolish at times.

❑ b. a smart aleck.

❑ c. a fairly wise decision maker.

❑ d. wiser than most of my friends.

2. *I think of myself as...*

❑ a. foolish at times.

❑ b. a smart aleck.

❑ c. a fairly wise decision maker.

❑ d. wiser than most of my friends.

3. *My wisest choices...*

❑ a. might be considered foolish compared to the choices of others.

❑ b. are a lot like the wise choices of others.

❑ c. lead to benefits that are visible to others.

❑ d. are wiser than those of most people.

4. *When criticized, I usually...*

❑ a. yell at the person who criticized me.

❑ b. throw a pity party and heap guilt on my critic.

❑ c. pay no attention to the criticism.

❑ d. listen to the criticism and change if appropriate.

5. *I usually show wisdom in this area of my life:*

❑ a. finances.

❑ b. relationships.

❑ c. sexual purity.

❑ d. time management.

❑ e. other (please be specific)

_____.

6. *I should exercise more wisdom in this area of my life:*

❑ a. finances.

❑ b. relationships.

❑ c. sexual purity.

❑ d. time management.

❑ e. other (please be specific)

_____.

research required

[think]

everywhere

[t a k e h o m e]

Driving Home the Point:

- It is easy to be wise after the events.

    (English proverb)

- Wisdom is only found in truth.

    (Johann Wolfgang von Goethe)

- The heart is wiser than the intellect.

    (J.G. Holland, *Katrina*)

- Some are weather-wise, some are otherwise.

    (Benjamin Franklin, *Poor Richard*)

- As for me, all I know is that I know nothing.

    (Socrates)

- The doorstep to the temple of wisdom is a knowledge of our own ignorance.

    (Charles Spurgeon, *Gleanings among the Sheaves*)

(Quotations taken from the Web site www.geocities.com)

Talking At Home:

Read James 1:5 with your family, and discuss these questions:

- **Who do you consider to be the wisest member of your family? Explain.**
- **Why is it important to understand what Christlike wisdom is?**

Work with your family to develop wisdom goals. These might include a set time for reading the Bible together or a prayer time devoted to asking God for wisdom.

Wisdom Beyond Belief

1 Kings 4:29-34;
Proverbs 1:1-7

6

Solomon Writes Many Proverbs

 KEY QUESTION: What does it mean to be wise?

 STUDY FOCUS: Students will gain a better understanding of true wisdom: what it is, where it comes from, and how they can exercise Christlike wisdom in their lives.

KEY VERSE: "The fear of the Lord is the beginning of wisdom, and knowledge of the Holy One is understanding" (Proverbs 9:10).

A Look at the Study

Study Sequence	Minutes	What Students Will Do	Classroom Supplies
Getting Started	10 to 15	**My Wiseguy**—Consider how the wisest people in their lives would handle tough situations.	Newsprint, markers, tape
Bible Story Exploration	10 to 15	**Solomon's Wisdom Exposed**—Create campaigns refuting Solomon's wisdom.	Bibles, "Proving Solomon's Wisdom" handouts (p. 52), newsprint, markers
	10 to 15	**Understanding Solomon's Wisdom**—Imagine how Solomon's wisdom affected his life.	Bibles, pens, paper, newsprint, marker, tape
Bible Application	10 to 15	**Wise Devotions**—Create devotions to help other teenagers understand and gain biblical wisdom.	Bibles
	5 to 10	**Being Wise**—Commit to being wise.	Bibles, newsprint, markers
	up to 5	**Faith Journal**—Respond in writing to an aspect of the Key Question.	Index cards, pens

Age-Level Insight

Teenagers often practice situational wisdom: Whatever situation they're in dictates whether or not they'll act wisely. Even though teens want to act wisely and seek out wise people, they still allow circumstances to steer them into doing unwise things. As you lead this study, consider challenging your students to write down what they believe about important issues (such as sex and alcohol) *before* they get caught in situations in which they'll have to decide what to do. If students think about issues before they feel caught in them, they'll be more likely to make choices that reflect Christlike wisdom.

NOTES

The people of Israel were not the only ones who were amazed by Solomon's wisdom; people in surrounding nations were also awed. Solomon was wiser than anyone else in the entire Middle East. People traveled hundreds of miles to witness his wisdom, and his fame spread throughout the known world.

Much of Solomon's wisdom was written down and preserved for future generations. Many of the three thousand proverbs he wrote are recorded in the book of Proverbs. Solomon also is credited with writing Song of Songs, Psalms 72 and 127, and possibly Ecclesiastes.

Proverbs 1:1-7 is something of an introduction to the book of Proverbs, describing its purpose and theme. Solomon's proverbs were not written as a showcase for his wisdom; rather, they were written for all the reasons stated in Proverbs 1:2-4. Solomon wrote so that God's people would be able to live better lives before God.

Wisdom is a key theme of the book of Proverbs; in fact, the word occurs fifty-one times in the book. In the Bible, the word carries the idea of "skill." Throughout the Old Testament, the same word is used to describe the skill of craftsmen. As used in Proverbs, however, "wisdom" also includes the concept of living skillfully according to God's plan, thereby avoiding moral failings.

An even more overarching theme is introduced in Proverbs 1:7: "The fear of the Lord is the beginning of knowledge." In this context, the word "fear" does not mean "fright"; instead it conveys the idea of reverence and submission to the lordship of God. We obtain true wisdom, then, when we honor God with our worship and submission to his will.

Throughout Proverbs, the wise and the simple are contrasted. The word "simple" occurs fifteen times in the book. The simple act on their own whims, but the wise seek God's view of things. Following God results in a peaceful and ultimately prosperous life.

Throughout most of his reign, Solomon applied God's principles of wisdom to ruling the people, and this resulted in peace and prosperity for the nation of Israel. Solomon's rule demonstrates the benefits a nation can enjoy when it faithfully follows God.

Getting Started

My Wiseguy

Before students arrive, write each of the following four situations on a separate sheet of newsprint, and post the four sheets in different parts of your meeting room.

• Your friend is stranded on a deserted island with three matches; an old, wet newspaper; a stick of gum; and a crowbar. Your friend must attract the attention of someone on the closest inhabited island, which is three islands away.

• You're out for a Sunday drive with your friend. As you're driving through a rough neighborhood, your car has a flat tire. Just as the two of you get out of the car to get the spare, a really big, intimidating man approaches you and asks if you have any spare change.

• You're at the grocery store with your friend, and two ladies begin fighting over a sale item. One lady has the last item in her cart, but the other lady wants it. The two of you watch as the argument unfolds.

• You and a friend are at an amusement park. For ninety minutes you've been waiting to ride the fastest roller coaster in the world. You're next in line for the front seat. When the gate opens, a woman behind you pushes past you and sits in your seat. When you ask her to move, she just stares blankly at you.

As students arrive, ask them to form four groups.

SAY **Today you're going to have a chance to talk about the wisest person you know. I'd like you to identify the wisest person you've ever met and then tell your group the person's name and why you think he or she is wise.**

Give students time to think and discuss. When they've finished, instruct each group to go to one of the situations posted on the wall. Then ask groups to read the situations and discuss how the wise people they know would respond to them. Then have groups each choose one of the wise people they talked about and create a role-play that shows how that person would handle the situation. When students are ready, have each group come forward and present its role-play.

ASK • **How would you define wisdom?**
• **How does someone get wisdom?**
• **What does it mean to be wise?**

SAY **Wise people are hard to find. Today I'd like you to discover how you can be really wise.**

Bible Story Exploration

Solomon's Wisdom Exposed

SAY **Solomon was the most famous wiseguy in the Bible. He was**

Last Week's **Impact**

As teenagers arrive, greet them warmly, and ask follow-up questions to review last week's study and Key Verse. Ask questions such as "Did you gain any wisdom last week?" and "How did you gain Christlike wisdom last week?"

If you used the Faith Journal option last week, take this time to return your students' index cards to them.

Tip From the **Trenches**

Be sure that only one group tackles each situation. If two groups want to discuss the same situation, ask them to work out a compromise, or ask them, "How would the wise people in your life handle this situation?"

Tip From the **Trenches**

If your group is highly creative, have students write their own situations. Then have them trade situations with another group and create role-plays showing how the wise people they know would respond to the situations they've been given.

Teacher SkillBuilder

Teenagers might not grasp the concept of fearing God, especially when they may have grown accustomed to fearing their parents or bullies at school. How can you help your students gain a healthy fear of God?

• Give them an accurate picture of God. Teenagers often lean toward fearing God more than trying to understand his grace. They may be quick to talk about how ashamed they feel because of their sins, but they often fail to grasp the grace that's theirs. Teach teenagers that, because of God's grace, their sins are forgiven.

• Give your students an accurate picture of fear. According to the Old Testament, fearing God doesn't mean being afraid of him; it means recognizing who God is and fearing his power and his righteousness.

Have students form groups of four. Give each foursome a copy of the "Proving Solomon's Wisdom" handout (p. 52). Ask groups to complete the first three steps of the handout. When they've finished, have groups split to form pairs. Instruct pairs to form new foursomes by joining a pair from a different group. Ask the new foursomes to discuss their findings so far.

SAY Now that you have all of your information together, proceed to the fourth step and create a campaign that helps others understand how unwise you think Solomon really was. Do your best to shape the information in a way that proves that Solomon wasn't wise.

Give foursomes newsprint and markers and time to create their campaigns. When they're ready, have them present the campaigns to the rest of the class. Ask the following questions after each presentation.

ASK • Are you persuaded that Solomon wasn't truly wise?
• Based on what you've been told, would you trust Solomon?

After all the foursomes have presented their campaigns, have students form a circle in the center of the meeting room.

ASK • What made Solomon wise?
• What effect did his wisdom have on him? What effect did it have on others?
• Why was wisdom so important to Solomon?
• Where does wisdom come from?
• What are the benefits of being wise? What are the drawbacks?
• What does it mean to be wise?

SAY Solomon knew that his wisdom didn't come from reading or from traveling. He knew that wisdom comes from fearing God. Solomon wasn't just smart; he was wise, and this wisdom was a gift from God.

Understanding Solomon's Wisdom

SAY Let's examine Solomon's wisdom to see what made it unique.

Have students form pairs, and give each pair a pen and paper. Tell students that you'd like them to reread 1 Kings 4:29-34 and Proverbs 1:1-7 and to list all of the qualities of Solomon's wisdom that they can glean from these Bible passages. When students have finished, have them gather in the center of the meeting room. Ask pairs to share their lists with the entire class. As they're sharing, write their ideas on a sheet of newsprint taped to the wall.

SAY You've done a great job of describing Solomon's wisdom. But even more important than describing Solomon's wisdom is understanding how that wisdom was reflected in his everyday life. Let's imagine for a moment how Solomon lived out the wisdom God gave him. I'd like you to imagine that you're Solomon's friend and you're watching him live out one of these qualities in his life. Write a story about the experience, including the situation, the quality he reveals in the situation, and the effect of this quality.

Give pairs time to write their stories. When they've finished, have pairs read their stories to the rest of the class.

ASK • How did these qualities affect Solomon's life?
• Why is practicing wisdom important?
• Is it possible to be wise in one area of your life and unwise in others?
• What does it mean to be wise?

SAY Solomon put his wisdom into practice. He possessed wisdom as well as the ability to use it in practical ways. It's important for us to not only seek wisdom, but also to use it.

Bible Application

Wise Devotions

Have students remain in their pairs. Instruct students to read the Key Verse, Proverbs 9:10, and to discuss the following questions with their partners.

ASK • What is the connection between knowing God and becoming wise?
• How does the fear of God help us become wise?
• What's the result of wisdom in our lives?
• What does it mean to be wise?

SAY The fear of God is the beginning of wisdom. But what effect does that wisdom have on our lives? Pretend that you've been asked to prepare a devotion about wisdom and to lead the devotion at a local event for high school students. You've been asked to tell the students the source of wisdom, how they can get biblical wisdom, and the effects of wisdom in the life of a believer. You may use anything that we've talked about today to help you prepare the devotion.

Give students time to create their devotions. When they've finished, have each pair join another pair to form a group of four.

SAY I'm going to give you a chance to practice your devotion. I'd like you to share your devotion with the pair you've just joined.

Give each pair a chance to share its devotion.

for **Younger** *teenagers*

Have younger teenagers imagine that they're aboard a ship that's hit a reef and is going to sink in an hour. Instruct them to choose three of Solomon's wise qualities to use in this situation and to explain their choices.

For Extra **Impact**

Invite a senior person from your church to speak about a time he or she acted wisely. Ask the person to explain how those actions have affected his or her life at the time as well as now.

ASK • What are the effects of wisdom in the life of a believer?
• How can we live out wisdom in our lives?
• What aspects of wisdom are the most difficult to live out?
• What effect does fearing God have on our relationship with him?
• What effect does wisdom have on our relationship with God?
• What does it mean to be wise?

SAY Wisdom is an easy word to toss around, but it can be a difficult concept to live out.

Being Wise

SAY All of this talk about wisdom is important, but if we don't make a commitment to seek wisdom and to act wisely, we're no further ahead. Wisdom isn't just an idea; it must be lived. Let's commit to being people who live wisely.

Have students each find a place in the room where they can be alone. Ask everyone to reread the Key Verse, Proverbs 9:10.

SAY Each of us faces an obstacle to living wisely. Some of us have trouble committing to God. Others of us simply take God very casually. Everyone's obstacle is different. I'd like you to think about the aspects of your life or your personality that prevent you from living wisely.

Have students form new pairs. Instruct students to say to their partners, "For me, the greatest obstacle to living wisely is..." then name the obstacle. When one member of the pair has done this, instruct that member's partner to repeat his or her partner's statement. Then have partners reverse roles and repeat the process.

SAY God longs for us to live wisely. We can do that if we commit to living for him in every situation we face, whether it's easy or tough.

Give each student a sheet of newsprint and a marker. Instruct everyone to write a statement of commitment to God at the top of the newsprint. Students might write, "I will do what I know God wants me to do in every situation." When students have finished, instruct them to write at the foot of their papers one word that describes an area of their lives in which they want to exercise true wisdom. When they've finished, have students find new partners and share what they've written. After students have shared, encourage partners to pray for each other's commitment throughout the upcoming week.

SAY If you think about it, you've come a long way today. You've learned where wisdom begins. And you've committed to being wise in one key area of your life.

Close the meeting with a short prayer for your students as they embark on their journey toward fearing God and gaining wisdom.

for OLDER teenagers

Ask older teenagers to pray every day that their wisdom will grow and to write a short, daily commentary about how they exercised wisdom. At the next study, have older teenagers read their commentaries.

Tip From the Trenches

As students are discussing the Key Verse, you might want to encourage them to take notes and incorporate key points in their devotions.

Faith Journal

Give each student an index card and a pen. Have teenagers write their names and their answers to the following question on their index cards:

- **Why is wisdom important?**

After teenagers have written their responses, ask them to return the cards to you. Before you meet with the group again, take time to write personal responses to your students on their index cards. You may want to keep a notebook or a box containing copies of these index cards as well as brief notes of prayer concerns and needs your students share using this assessment tool.

For more information about the Faith Journal option, refer to page 5 of the Introduction.

Tip From the Trenches

To help strengthen the connection between church and home, photocopy the "Taking It Home" page at the end of this study, and either distribute copies to students before they leave or mail them to their homes. Encourage students to complete the reading, activities, and discussion with their families during the coming week.

Proving Solomon's Wisdom

Word about Solomon's wisdom has spread. Apparently some people think he's wise, and others think he's a crackpot. You're the leaders of the Scandal Post, a sensationalist Israelite newspaper. You're out to prove that Solomon isn't as wise as people think he is.

- **Step 1:** Read 1 Kings 4:29-34 to see what people are saying about Solomon. Then set out to do your job. What are people saying about Solomon in this passage that you want to disprove? How will you disprove it?

- **Step 2:** Read 1 Kings 3:16-28. This passage describes an instance in which people say Solomon used the wisdom that God gave him. Take another look at the passage. How can you disprove it? What information can you derive from this passage that proves that Solomon *isn't* as wise as people say he is?

research required

- **Step 3:** Read Proverbs 1:1-7, in which Solomon tells others how to be wise. These are pretty outrageous instructions! Reread Solomon's instructions and use his own words to prove that Solomon isn't really teaching about wisdom.

- **Step 4:** Now that you've got all your information together, it's your job to get it to the people. Create a campaign designed to prove that Solomon isn't wise. Make your case, using whatever means you choose.

Driving Home the Point:

"Experience comes from what we have done. Wisdom comes from what we have done badly."

(Theodore Levitt, Harvard Business School, as quoted in www.sermonillustrations.com)

Talking At Home:

Read 1 Corinthians 1:20-31 with your family, and discuss these questions:

- **How can we know when someone is wise?**
- **What are some important qualities in a wise person?**
- **What does it take to gain wisdom?**

At an evening meal at which mashed potatoes are served, ask family members to shape their potatoes into something that represents the wisest person they've ever met. When they've made their shapes, have family members tell why they think the people they've chosen are wise. As family members share, write down their responses. Then read the responses to the family. Ask them which quality or trait they want to adopt.

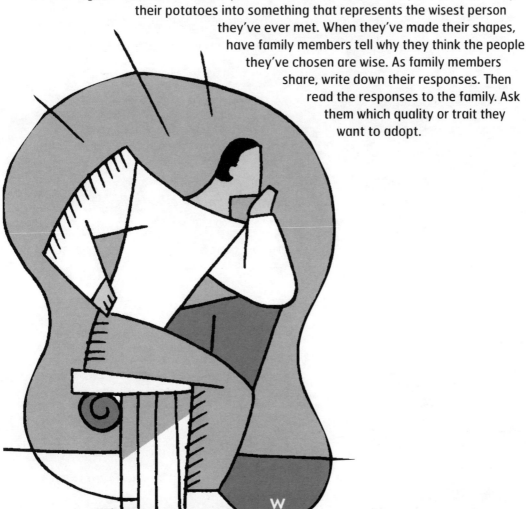

Permission to photocopy this handout from FaithWeaver™ Youth Bible Studies granted for local church use. Copyright © FaithWeaver™ www.faithweaver.com

Divine Devotion

1 Kings 11:1-13

7

Solomon Turns Away From God

 KEY QUESTION: What does it mean to be devoted to God?

 STUDY FOCUS: Students will explore the benefits of being devoted to God and determine ways they can remain devoted to God throughout their lives.

KEY VERSES: "Trust in the Lord with all your heart and lean not on your own understanding; in all your ways acknowledge him, and he will make your paths straight" (Proverbs 3:5-6).

A Look at the Study

Study Sequence	Minutes	What Students Will Do	Classroom Supplies
Getting Started	10 to 15	**Speed Advice**—Advise teenagers who have rebelled.	"Teenagers Gone Wrong" handouts (pp. 61-62), pens
Bible Story Exploration	15 to 20	**Sitting With Solomon**—In a role-play, try to persuade Solomon not to rebel.	Bibles, newsprint, markers
	10 to 15	**Staying Devoted**—List things Solomon did to turn away from God.	Bibles, newsprint, markers, tape, self-adhesive address labels
Bible Application	10 to 15	**The Devoted I Know**—Describe the devoted people they know.	Newsprint, markers
	up to 5	**My Path of Devotion**—Create a wall of ideas for ways to remain devoted.	Bibles, index cards, markers, transparent tape
	up to 5	**Faith Journal**—Respond in writing to an aspect of the Key Question.	Index cards, pens

Age-Level Insight

Being devoted to God is difficult for teenagers. They face daily assaults on their senses calling them to give their entire selves to the latest fad or trend. As you lead this study, don't just give students information; encourage them to use what they've learned to remain devoted to God throughout their entire lives. Encourage students to identify the areas of their lives in which they are less devoted to God and to make those areas real targets of prayer. If they feel open to it, encourage students to seek spiritual counsel about these areas.

NOTES

God had forbidden David to build a temple because David had shed blood as he fought to establish the kingdom of Israel (1 Chronicles 28:2-3). However, David did make preparations for a temple to be built, and he commissioned his son Solomon to make sure that it happened (1 Chronicles 22:2-11).

Once the Temple was built, Solomon dedicated it with a magnificent prayer (1 Kings 8:23-53). He praised God's power, goodness, and mercy. He asked God to hear, forgive, and bless his people. After that prayer, God appeared to Solomon and reaffirmed his promise to establish an heir of David on the throne forever if Solomon and his descendants continued to walk before God in "integrity of heart and uprightness" (1 Kings 9:4-5). However, God also issued a warning: If Solomon or his sons turned away from the Lord and served other gods, God would reject them and make Israel an object of ridicule among all peoples (1 Kings 9:6-7). So Solomon was duly warned.

Solomon's wisdom and Israel's prosperity made Solomon enormously wealthy. First Kings 10:14-29 describes some of his possessions, including huge amounts of gold, a fleet of ships, hundreds of chariots, and thousands of horses—all in spite of the fact that the accumulation of large numbers of horses and vast amounts of gold and silver was expressly forbidden in Deuteronomy 17:16-17.

Solomon also enjoyed foreign women. Again, this was against God's wishes. The king of Israel was not to take many wives for himself because they would lead him astray (Deuteronomy 17:17). Solomon had seven hundred wives and three hundred concubines. But having foreign wives was even worse than having many wives, and many of Solomon's wives were from nations whose people Israelites were expressly forbidden to marry (1 Kings 11:1-2). Indeed the wives led him astray. After such an illustrious beginning to his reign and many years of faithfulness and prosperity, Solomon turned to worshipping the gods of his foreign wives. He not only worshipped those gods, but he also built altars for them, an act that no doubt encouraged the people of Israel to worship them as well. So the wise Solomon not only turned away from God, but he led his people astray as well.

Solomon's wisdom didn't do him any good when he neglected to heed it. The next time God spoke to Solomon, it was to tell him that the kingdom would be torn from Solomon's son. Only as an honor to David was Solomon allowed to maintain the kingdom until his death.

Getting Started

Speed Advice

Before students arrive, make four copies of the "Teenagers Gone Wrong" handout (pp. 61-62), and circle a different story on each handout.

SAY Today we're going to examine why people turn away from God and how we can remain devoted to God. First let's think about what it takes to stay devoted to something.

Have teenagers form four groups, and give each group a pen and a copy of the handout. Ask each group to read the circled story and to then write advice for remaining devoted in the situation described there. (Students may write on the reverse side of the handout.) When groups have finished, have them trade their handouts with another group and repeat the process, offering advice relevant to the story circled on the new handout. If you have time, repeat the process until all groups have offered advice for each situation. Have groups retrieve their original handouts and choose which advice they feel is best for the people in their stories. Then ask groups to tell which advice they've chosen and to explain why.

ASK • What does it take to remain devoted to something?
• What does it mean to be devoted to God?
• What are the benefits of being devoted to God?

SAY It can be really easy to go astray. Today we're going to talk about how we can remain committed to God.

Bible Story Exploration

Sitting With Solomon

Have students form pairs.

SAY Imagine that you're Solomon and you've made a series of really bad choices. Everyone in Israel thinks you're really smart, but God knows you've made life-threatening decisions. I'd like you to imagine that you're having a discussion with Solomon.

Discuss - ask question on 58 Write down answer

Instruct students to read 1 Kings 11:1-13. Assign half of the pairs to play the role of Solomon's friends and the other half to play the role of Solomon. Instruct students to prepare a debate about Solomon's choice to worship other gods. Give pairs newsprint and markers to record their ideas and arguments. Encourage students to use what they've learned from the Bible passage. When they're ready, instruct students who are playing Solomon's friends to stand on one side of the room and those who are playing Solomon to stand on the opposite side. Place two chairs facing each other in the center of the room. Ask one pair from each side to come forward, and invite one person from each pair to sit in each chair.

Last Week's Impact

As teenagers arrive, greet them warmly, and ask follow-up questions to review last week's study and Key Verse. Ask questions such as "What does it mean to be wise?" and "How did you act wisely last week?"

If you used the Faith Journal option last week, take this time to return your students' index cards to them.

For Extra Impact

If you know teenagers who have struggled with remaining devoted to their families or to God, invite them to share their stories either at the beginning of the opening activity or as a substitute for it.

for OLDER teenagers

Have older students each find a partner and share times they've had trouble remaining devoted to God. After students have shared, begin the study with a time of prayer in which students pray for their partners.

SAY **If you're Solomon's friend, I'd like you to confront Solomon about the choices he's made. If you're Solomon, I'd like you to defend your choices. When you're stumped, you may either change places with your partner, or you may ask a new team to take your place.**

Give students time to get their debate going. During the debate you might want to toss in ideas for either side to use. For example, to students playing the role of Solomon, you might say, "You're a powerful man; no one can tell you what to do or who to worship." And to those playing Solomon's friends you might say, "This is your friend. He's chosen to worship other gods, even though God has appeared to him twice."

After everyone has participated in the debate, ask students to gather in the center of the room.

ASK • **Why do you think Solomon decided to worship other gods?**
• **Why was it dangerous for Solomon to worship other gods?**
• **What effect did Solomon's choice have on his relationship with God?**
• **What does Solomon's choice say about his devotion to God?**
• **What does it mean to be devoted to God?**

SAY **Solomon took his closeness to God for granted and chose to worship other gods. This choice had serious consequences. When we lose our devotion to God, we put our relationship with God at risk, and we lose our sense of intimacy with him—even though God never turns away from us.**

Staying Devoted

SAY **Solomon's choices changed his life. Instead of remaining devoted to God, he chose to worship other gods to see what they had to offer. This choice put him out of favor with God. Let's examine Solomon's choices and consider choices he might have made instead.**

Have students form pairs, and give each pair a sheet of newsprint and a marker. Instruct pairs to reread 1 Kings 11:1-13 and to make a list of the things Solomon did that led him away from God. When they've finished, have students gather in the center of the meeting room and read their lists aloud. As students are reading, write their responses on a sheet of newsprint taped to the wall of your meeting room. When all the pairs have reported, have students review the list.

ASK • **How easy was it for Solomon to walk away from God?**
• **What does it mean to be devoted to God?**
• **Why do some people choose not to be devoted to God?**
• **What effect does devotion to God have on our lives?**

SAY **Let's suppose that you're a member of a top-notch advertising team that has been hired to create an ad** campaign encouraging people to remain devoted to God. Use this list to help you think of ideas for bumper stickers that will inspire people to remain devoted to God.

Give each pair a sheet of newsprint, two self-adhesive address labels, and markers. Instruct pairs to list their ideas on the newsprint and then to write their two best ideas on the address labels. When they've finished, have students stick the bumper stickers to their partners' backs.

ASK
• **What would you think if you were in traffic and you read one of these bumper stickers for the first time?**
• **What message do you think Solomon's lack of devotion sent to those around him?**
• **What does it mean to be devoted to God?**
• **What effect do you think Solomon's lack of devotion had on his gift of wisdom?**
• **Why is staying devoted to God so important?**

Bible Application

The Devoted I Know

SAY **Solomon lost favor with God because he didn't remain devoted to God. All of us have known people who have remained devoted to God throughout their lives, even in the midst of tough circumstances. I'd like you to think about those people now.**

Give each student a sheet of newsprint and a marker. Instruct students to write the names of people they consider to be extremely devoted to God. Tell students that these people can be their relatives or people unrelated to them. If students have a difficult time thinking of people they know, instruct them to write the names of people they've heard of. When they've finished, have students share their lists with their partners from the previous activity.

SAY **Now I'd like you to think of the qualities that helped these people remain devoted to God. Make a quick list of those qualities.**

After students have had time to make their lists, have them form trios and share their lists.

SAY **Now I'd like you to combine all of these ideas to create a life-size drawing of a devoted person. You may draw a simple stick figure, but I'd like you to somehow incorporate the qualities of a devoted person into the drawing. For example, you could write the qualities next to the parts of the body that might relate to those qualities. For example, you could write "thinking pure thoughts" next to the stick figure's head.**

Give each trio a sheet of newsprint and markers and plenty of time to draw.

When they've finished, have them display and explain their drawings.

ASK • How have these people benefited by their devotion to God?
• What effects has their devotion to God had on you?
• What struggles have these people faced in remaining devoted to God?
• Based on the qualities you see in these people, what do you think it means to be devoted to God?

SAY All of us know of people who have remained devoted to God; in fact, they're all around us. They are good reminders that we face the same challenges that Solomon faced, but with God's help, we can remain devoted to him.

My Path of Devotion

SAY The people you've thought of stand like pillars in your life. You can turn to them or remember their example when you don't know how to remain devoted to God. Each of us can learn something about being devoted to God by watching how these people live. In the same way, we need to strive to be devoted to God so that others may mirror our example.

Give each student a marker and several index cards. Instruct students to write on each index card one way to remain devoted to God. When they've finished, give students as many pieces of transparent tape as they need.

SAY Now I'd like you to tape your index cards to the wall to make a whole wall of ideas for remaining devoted to God.

After students have taped their cards to the wall, ask students to each find a partner. Ask pairs to reread the first part of the Key Verses: "Trust in the Lord with all your heart " (Proverbs 3:5a) and to then say a prayer for their partners that is based on this part of the Key Verses. For example, someone might pray, "Lord, please help Steve trust in you with all his heart by reading your Word every day." When students have finished praying, pray aloud for your students' attempts to trust in God with all their hearts.

Faith Journal

Give each student an index card and a pen. Have teenagers write their names and their answers to the following question on their index cards:

• Why is devotion to God important?

After teenagers have written their responses, ask them to return the index cards to you. Before you meet with the group again, take time to write personal responses to your students on their index cards. You may want to keep a notebook or a box containing copies of these index cards as well as brief notes of prayer concerns and needs your students share using this assessment tool.

For more information about the Faith Journal option, refer to page 5 of the Introduction.

Tip From the **Trenches**

To help strengthen the connection between church and home, photocopy the "Taking It Home" page at the end of this study, and either distribute copies to students before they leave or mail them to their homes. Encourage students to complete the reading, activities, and discussion with their families during the coming week.

[t h i n k]

STORY 1

Jenny has been a favorite at the ballet school for three years. It has been obvious since she began lessons that her natural ability and her determination set her above everyone else. After her second year of classes, the head instructor asked Jenny to teach some of the lower-level classes. Jenny was thrilled. Then one day, the head instructor disagreed with Jenny's decision to hold a mini-recital for the younger students. (Jenny had advertised the recital before asking permission.) After a mild blowup, things settled down, and Jenny resumed teaching.

But recently Jenny has been hanging out at the ballet school less and less. She's missed a lot of her classes, and the school has canceled the classes she was teaching because Jenny has given up on them.

STORY 2

Larry was the star of the soccer team. Besides scoring most of the goals, he was the team's leader in every way. When morale was low, his teammates could count on Larry to cheer them up. He also persuaded youth pastors to lead the team in a devotion before every game.

A few weeks ago, Larry had a really bad game. He scored only one goal, and he got into a fight with one of his teammates. Since then, Larry's performance has gone downhill. His attitude is bad, he argues with the coach, and he's rarely on time. Larry has told his friends that he hates soccer and wants to quit.

research required

[think]

STORY 3

Crystal was her parents' favorite child. They loved to buy her stuffed animals and cute clothes. Then Crystal's parents separated and divorced. Since then, Crystal has been living life on the edge.

First she got involved with the wrong people at school. They aren't really bad; they just don't go to church, and they like to stay out late on the weekends. After a few weeks, Crystal stopped coming home on Friday night. When her mom realized that she wasn't staying with friends, she confronted Crystal. Since then, Crystal has been distancing herself even more from her parents, siblings, and most of her friends.

STORY 4

Aaron is the smartest person in his class. Even though he's a sophomore, his teachers are already sure he will be the valedictorian of his class. Aaron isn't only smart; he's also kind and generous. Last year it was Aaron's idea to lead his youth group to reach out to homeless people during Thanksgiving.

Recently Aaron has been reading books about the philosophies of other religions and beliefs. His appearance has changed; he wears all black and has grown his hair to be really long. During the past two months, Aaron's attendance at church and youth group has been sporadic. When his friend Phil approached him about his attendance, Aaron said, "You know, Christianity is great for weak and small-minded people. But for those of us who are smart, it just doesn't make much sense."

research required

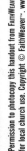

Taking It Home

Talking About It

Driving Home the Point:

"The motto of every missionary, whether preacher, printer, or schoolmaster, ought to be 'Devoted for life.' "

(Adoniram Judson, *To The Golden Shore: The Life of Adoniram Judson*, as quoted in sermonillustrations.com)

Talking At Home:

Read Isaiah 42:14-17 with your family, and discuss these questions:

- **Why is it tempting to trust things other than God with important issues?**
- **What prevents us from being devoted to God?**

Go to a local park, and silently walk around the park once. (If you're not near a park, consider walking around the block.) As you begin walking, ask family members to think of times they've shown extreme devotion to God.

After walking around the park once, ask family members to share the times they thought of. Then ask family members to think of a time they weren't devoted to God. Walk around the park silently again, then stop and ask family members to share those times. Finally discuss ideas for helping each family member remain devoted to God.

The Root of Division

1 Kings 11:28–12:24

8

 KEY QUESTION: What happens when we rebel against God?

 STUDY FOCUS: Students will discuss why they rebel against God and how they can obey him when they are tempted to rebel.

KEY VERSE: "If my people, who are called by my name, will humble themselves and pray and seek my face and turn from their wicked ways, then will I hear from heaven and will forgive their sin and will heal their land" (2 Chronicles 7:14).

A Look at the Study

Study Sequence	Minutes	What Students Will Do	Classroom Supplies
Getting Started	10 to 15	**Rebellion Soap Operas**—Create soap operas about rebellion.	"Soap Opera Script Outlines" handouts (pp. 72-73)
Bible Story Exploration	10 to 15	**Divided Loyalties**—Write letters to friends in the other half of the divided kingdom.	Bibles, newsprint, markers
	10 to 15	**The Heart of Rebellion**—Create artwork depicting key words of the Key Verse.	Bibles, newsprint, markers, tape, index cards
Bible Application	10 to 15	**Opportunities and Ideas**—Discuss the opportunities for rebelling that they face every day.	Index cards, markers
	5 to 10	**Personal Rebellion**—Ask forgiveness for their acts of rebellion.	Bibles
	up to 5	**Faith Journal**—Respond in writing to an aspect of the Key Question.	Index cards, pens

Age-Level Insight

Rebellion differs from teenager to teenager. Younger students might not understand what it means to rebel since they may not have had much experience. Older teenagers may be more adept at rebelling openly than younger teenagers.

Students need to observe people in their daily lives who are actually obeying God. As you lead this study, point out people in your church or in the media who consistently obey God. Encourage students to consider those people when they struggle with obedience.

NOTES

Soon after God's pronouncement that the kingdom of Israel would be taken from Solomon's descendants, God raised up enemies against Israel. They never defeated Israel but caused problems for Solomon for the remainder of his life. But they were not his biggest problem. Jeroboam, one of Solomon's trusted officials, turned against him. And God was on Jeroboam's side.

Ahijah the prophet, speaking for the Lord, predicted the division of the kingdom and gave leadership of ten tribes to Jeroboam. A careful reading of 1 Kings 11:31-32 shows that in demonstrating the division to Jeroboam, Ahijah started with twelve pieces of cloth, representing the twelve tribes of Israel, but ended up using only eleven in his illustration. There are several possible explanations for this. One is that the Levites were a tribe but had no land allotment, so Ahijah didn't count them in the division of land. Another possibility is that he simply included Simeon as part of Judah because the tribe was small and had essentially been swallowed up in the large tribe of Judah.

God's offer to Jeroboam echoed both God's promise to David in 2 Samuel 7:12-16 and David's charge to Solomon in 1 Kings 2:1-4. If the king would walk in God's ways and be obedient to him, God would be with him. This theme of God's blessing in return for obedience and his punishment in return for rebellion continually recurred as God dealt with the kings chosen to rule his people.

When Solomon learned that God had chosen Jeroboam to succeed him, Solomon tried to kill Jeroboam. He acted much as Saul, Israel's first king, had acted when he tried to kill David, the one anointed to replace Saul. Both of these attempts stand in contrast to David's refusal to kill Saul even when he had the opportunity. The wise Solomon had lost all trust in the God who had given him so much, and he had no intention of obeying him. Thus he lost God's blessing on his life and on his kingdom.

Rehoboam, the son whom Solomon chose to succeed him as king, apparently didn't inherit Solomon's wisdom. Instead of listening to the wise counsel of Solomon's advisers and the pleas of his people, Rehoboam chose to follow the prompting of his young friends. Instead of winning the favor of the people by lightening their tax load, he increased it in order to fill his own coffers.

When the ten tribes decided to reject Rehoboam, he made an attempt to bring them into line by sending Adoniram, who was in charge of forced labor, to the people. But the people stoned Adoniram. Rehoboam then gathered an army and prepared to attack Jeroboam and Israel. God spoke through the prophet Shemaiah to prevent the 180,000-man army of Judah from attacking Israel. In contrast to his father, whose later life was characterized by disobedience, Rehoboam obeyed God this time, and the split between the two parts of the kingdom was complete.

Getting Started

Rebellion Soap Operas

As students arrive, have them form trios.

SAY We all have to deal with rebellion. Either we choose to rebel, or someone else's rebellion affects our lives. Your job as a trio is to create a quick skit based on the script outline I am about to give you.

Give each trio one section of the "Soap Opera Script Outlines" handout (pp. 72-73). Ask each trio to create a one-minute soap opera based on its assigned outline. Encourage students to overact as they prepare their skits. Tell them they have five minutes to prepare.

When everyone has finished, have each trio present its soap opera to the rest of the class. Ask the following questions after each trio's presentation.

ASK • What does this soap opera say about people who rebel?
• What did the people in this soap opera rebel against?

When all the trios have presented, have everyone gather in the center of the meeting room.

ASK • Why do people rebel against each other?
• Why do people rebel against God?
• What happens when we rebel against God?

SAY Rebelling against God can cause a lot of trouble. Today we're going to talk about the consequences of rebellion against God and ways to avoid rebelling.

Bible Story Exploration

Divided Loyalties

SAY It's one thing to rebel and damage your relationship with God. But when rebellion hurts an entire nation, many more people suffer. Let's explore the Israelites' rebellion against God and the consequences of that rebellion.

Instruct students to form groups of four or five. Ask groups to read 1 Kings 11:28–12:24.

SAY Let's review what happened in this passage. God sent the prophet Ahijah to Jeroboam with this message: God was going to take most of the kingdom of Israel from Solomon's son. Because God had promised David, Solomon's father, that the kingdom would stay in his family line, he would let Solomon's family keep two tribes of the kingdom. But the

Last Week's Impact

As teenagers arrive, greet them warmly, and ask follow-up questions to review last week's study and Key Verses. Ask questions such as "How did you stay devoted to God last week?" and "What benefits did you realize by staying devoted to God?"

If you used the Faith Journal option last week, take this time to return your students' index cards to them.

Teaching about obedience can be difficult. How can you help your students understand the issue of obedience without stepping on toes at home?

• Use God's Word by citing instances in the Bible in which God asks us to obey him. And if you're mentioning specific things, be sure to reference those (but be sure not to take Scriptures out of context!). If you say something that causes controversy at home, students will have the reference and will be able to discuss that with their parents.

• Teach grace. Tell students that God's laws apply to everyone but so does God's forgiveness. Tell students that if they mess up, God loves to forgive them and set them free from the bondage of sin when they ask for his forgiveness.

Have students form two groups and go to separate rooms. Tell students to pretend that they're living in their new kingdom but have the ability to send one video message to their peers in the other kingdom. Give them the resources to record a message about their new kingdom. When they've finished, have groups trade videotapes and watch them. Then debrief using the questions in the study.

rest of the tribes would leave the kingdom, and Jeroboam would be their king.

SAY **Why did God do this? Because the Israelites, under Solomon's leadership, were worshipping other gods. They had turned against God and his laws.**

Eventually, Solomon died and his son Rehoboam became king. Rehoboam followed some bad advice and refused to show kindness to his people, so God's prediction came true. Ten of the tribes rebelled against Rehoboam and made Jeroboam their king.

I'd like you to imagine that you're either a member of one of the ten tribes that rebelled against Solomon's son or a member of one of the two tribes still under his rule. With your group, review the passage you just read, then write a letter to a friend, describing your situation. Tell your friend what happened to your part of the kingdom, why it happened, and how it has affected your life.

Give each group a sheet of newsprint and a marker. Allow groups time to complete their letters. When they've finished, have groups read their letters to the rest of the class.

ASK • **What do you think it was like for the Israelites to have their national identity change so much when the kingdom divided?**
• **Why did the kingdoms divide?**
• **How do you think you would have felt if you had lived through this experience?**
• **What happens when we rebel against God?**

SAY **The Israelites experienced a dramatic ripping apart of life as they knew it. When their land and their politics were divided into two separate kingdoms, their lives must have changed dramatically. All this upheaval came because Solomon rebelled against God and led the people of Israel to do the same.**

The Heart of Rebellion

SAY **Rebellion against God tore apart the kingdom of Israel, just as our rebellion can make us feel as if we've torn apart our relationship with God. But God never forsakes us or gives up on us. Let's investigate what the Bible says about God's response to our rebellion.**

Instruct students to form four groups of equal size. (If your class is large, form groups in multiples of four. Then double up the assignments on the following page.) Give each group markers and a sheet of newsprint. Ask groups to read 2 Chronicles 7:14.

SAY **This verse tells us specifically how to restore our relationship with God after we've rebelled. I'd like you to** consider what each of the challenging statements in this verse means.

Assign each group one of the following words or phrases from the Key Verse: "humble," "pray," "seek my face," and "turn from wicked ways." Explain that you'd like each group to draw a picture depicting the word or phrase it has been assigned. Tell groups to tape their art to the wall when they've finished.

When groups have finished, have students gather in the center of the meeting room. Give each group one index card and a marker. Ask groups to walk around the room, studying the art on the wall, and choose which picture they'd want to buy. Ask groups to make their choices based on how well they feel the assigned word or phrase was portrayed.

ASK
- **Which word or phrase in this verse is the easiest to live out?**
- **Why do you think God asks us to take these steps after rebellion?**
- **How does rebellion affect our relationship with God?**
- **How does turning back to God affect our relationship with him?**
- **What happens when we rebel against God?**

SAY **The Bible makes it clear that rebellion against God is wrong and it always has dramatic consequences. But if we turn back to God and acknowledge him, he'll always forgive us and restore our relationship with him.**

Bible Application

Opportunities and Ideas

SAY **Throughout its history Israel has rebelled against God and then sought to restore that relationship. This is very much like us. Every day we face opportunities to rebel against God. And sometimes it seems impossible to do the right thing.**

Have students form groups of three. Give each trio markers and several index cards. Ask trios to think of daily opportunities to rebel against God and to describe one on each card. For example, students might list gossiping, yelling at their parents, or watching questionable movies. Give students time to write their ideas. When they've finished, stack the index cards.

Distribute more cards to the trios, and ask them to write ideas to prevent themselves from rebelling against God. For example, students might list prayer or talking with friends when they're tempted. Remind students to write one idea on each card. Gather all of these cards, and place them in another stack.

Have students gather in the center of the meeting room.

for OLDER teenagers

Instead of asking older students to draw pictures, have them write their assigned word or phrase in the middle of a sheet of newsprint then surround it with words or phrases that amplify it. For example, students who are assigned the phrase "seek my face" might write "Keep up with devotions" and "Give up my will for God's." Have groups present their word collages to the entire class, then ask students to decide which action listed in the Key Verse is the most difficult to do in today's society and explain why.

for Younger teenagers

Inflate at least forty balloons. Write one of the following words or phrases on each balloon: "humble," "pray," "seek my face," "turn from wicked ways," "disobey God," "sin," and "ignore God's laws." Explain that you'd like the students to pop as many balloons as possible in five seconds. Give students the signal to begin, and give them five seconds to pop the balloons. (Make sure that several balloons remain intact.) When students have settled down, ask them to form groups of four, pick up an inflated balloon, and read the words on it. Then ask each foursome to create a rap based on that word or phrase. When they're ready, have groups present their raps.

SAY It can be tough to remain devoted to God. Let's talk about some of the ways you're tempted to rebel against God. I'll read an idea from the stack describing daily opportunities to rebel. Then I'll ask you to discuss times you faced that opportunity. Then I'll choose a card from the second stack and ask how you would put that idea into practice when facing the situation described on the first card. So, for example, if you have the opportunity to watch a questionable movie, and the idea is to be accountable, you will describe how that idea will help you when faced with the opportunity to watch a questionable movie.

Begin reading the situations and the ideas for not rebelling. Be sure to allow students time to discuss instances in which they faced those situations and all of their ideas for preventing rebellion.

Finally, ask everyone to find a partner and discuss the following questions.

ASK • When have you faced an opportunity to rebel against God and taken it? What was the result?
• What competes with God for your devotion? How powerful is that competition?
• In your experience, what's the best way to restore your relationship with God after you've rebelled against him?
• What happens when we rebel against God?

SAY Rebelling is an easy choice that has a lasting impact. Let's be people who commit to remaining devoted to God. And when we've messed up, let's come back to God and accept his grace and forgiveness.

Personal Rebellion

SAY Whether we want to admit it or not, all of us have rebelled against God. Maybe today you're rebelling against God. Or maybe you've rebelled against God in the past, and you want to ask for forgiveness.

Have students find a place in the room where they can each be alone. Instruct students to think about an act of rebellion for which they'd like to ask forgiveness. Give students sufficient time to identify their acts of rebellion, then ask everyone to find a partner. Instruct pairs to read the Key Verse, 2 Chronicles 7:14, to each other.

SAY When we rebel, the best thing for us to do is to turn to God and ask for forgiveness. He longs to set us free from the consequences of our rebellion. Let's take some time right now and ask for forgiveness.

Instruct partners to discuss their acts of rebellion, then give them time to pray for each other. When they've finished, have students gather in the center of the meeting room, and ask volunteers to share what they prayed about. When students share, verbally affirm their choice to share their struggles and to ask for forgiveness. After a few minutes of sharing, close the meeting by asking God to help your students remain devoted to him.

Faith Journal

Give each student an index card and a pen. Have teenagers write their names and their answers to the following question on their index cards:

- **Why is rebelling against God wrong?**

After teenagers have written their responses, ask them to return the cards to you. Before you meet with the group again, take time to write personal responses to your students on their index cards. You may want to keep a notebook or a box containing copies of these index cards as well as brief notes of prayer concerns and needs your students share using this assessment tool.

For more information about the Faith Journal option, refer to page 5 of the Introduction.

Tip From
the **Trenches**

To help strengthen the connection between church and home, photocopy the "Taking It Home" page at the end of this study, and either distribute copies to students before they leave or mail them to their homes. Encourage students to complete the reading, activities, and discussion with their families during the coming week.

Soap Opera Script Outlines

Broken Hearts Can Mend

Today's drama calls for Brent and Sheila to confront Heather, who's fallen in love with a local pig farmer. Heather is on parole for grooming pets without the permission of their owners. One condition of her parole forbids her from associating with animals or animal owners of any kind. At first, Heather tried denying that she was involved with the farmer, but the constant smell of pig slop gave her away. Plus, Heather has been spotted carrying pigs with her wherever she goes. Brent and Sheila want Heather to drop the pig farmer and get her life back in order, or they may threaten to tell Heather's parole officer about her involvement with the farmer.

Holding Strong in LOVE

Bill and Kelli have been best friends since kindergarten. In today's script, Bill and Kelli fall in love at the arts and crafts fair. Kelli realizes she's in love when she and Bill are eating corn dogs together and she looks up and sees Bill's chin smeared with mustard. The problem is that Bill is engaged to Elizabeth, who owns the corn dog stand. Also, the rules of the arts and crafts fair forbid attendees to date one another. Bill has a big decision to make. He chooses to date Kelli and refuses to return his corn dog.

research required

Rebellious Lives, Shattered Dreams

Harry has been addicted to Twinkies for the past three years. The Twinkies have taken a serious toll on his health. He's lost his job, his family has disowned him, and his fiancee has warned him to shape up or she's leaving him. Patti (Harry's fiancee) has asked Tim and Jack to confront Harry about his Twinkie problem. The two men confront Harry in the glue factory where Harry works. A fight ensues, and Harry accidentally gets shoved into a huge vat of glue.

Teen Life

Sarah's parents have asked her to till the garden. Instead, she goes to a party with her best friend, Lisa. A camera crew from the local TV station does a story on the high-society people at the party. Sarah arrives home and is confronted by her parents, who have watched the news and have seen her at the party.

[think]

research required

Talking About It

Driving Home the Point:

"Great is Thy faithfulness, Lord, unto me!"

(Thomas O. Chisholm, "Great Is Thy Faithfulness")

Talking At Home:

Read Matthew 28:16-20 with your family, and discuss these questions:

- **What does it mean to teach others to obey God's commands?**
- **Why is obedience important?**
- **What's the best way to teach others to obey God?**

Label a container "Ways I've Obeyed God This Week." Place index cards next to the container. Ask family members to use the index cards to describe instances in which they obey God during the upcoming week. Ask family members to be as anonymous as possible. For example, you might want to instruct them to use the family computer to type their descriptions. At the end of the week, meet with your family and read the cards. Spend time praising God for giving you and your family the strength to obey him.

Total Trust

1 Kings 17:7-24

9

 KEY QUESTION: What does it mean to trust God completely?

 STUDY FOCUS: Students will understand that they can trust God to meet all their needs.

KEY VERSES: "So do not worry, saying, 'What shall we eat?' or 'What shall we drink?' or 'What shall we wear?' For the pagans run after all of these things, and your heavenly Father knows that you need them. But seek first his kingdom and his righteousness, and all these things will be given to you as well" (Matthew 6:31-33).

A Look at the Study

Study Sequence	Minutes	What Students Will Do	Classroom Supplies
Getting Started	10 to 15	**What I've Got**—See what they can buy with a limited amount of cash.	"Let's Go Shopping!" handout (p. 82), calculators, pencils
Bible Story Exploration	15 to 20	**A Widow's Trust**—Disprove then defend the miracle described in the Bible story.	Bibles, newsprint, markers
	10 to 15	**Simple Study in Trust**—Discuss the Key Verses and try to explain them to others.	Bibles, newsprint, markers
Bible Application	up to 10	**Extreme Trust**—Commit to seeking God's kingdom first in their lives.	Paper, pens, jar
	up to 5	**Faith Journal**—Respond in writing to an aspect of the Key Question.	Index cards, pens

Age-Level Insight

Most teenagers' physical and material needs are met by their parents. However, some students may feel that their intangible needs are not being met—their need for love, for friends, or for security, for example. Even teenagers in healthy homes have needs that their families can't meet. This study will help your teenagers understand that they can trust God to meet all their needs. Remind students that they can also seek help from their pastors or friends when their needs aren't being met.

NOTES

Under Rehoboam's rule, "Judah did evil in the sight of the Lord" (1 Kings 14:22), and this pattern continued under most of the kings of Judah and Israel who followed. In today's passage, the king of Israel is Ahab, and he did more evil than any of the kings who had come before him (1 Kings 16:30). Because of that evil, God sent judgment on Israel in the form of a drought. The drought was also likely intended to show the powerlessness of Baal, the god worshipped in Israel, who was thought to be responsible for giving rain. In addition, God sent the prophet Elijah away from the land, leaving the Israelites without God's word and blessing. Elijah camped near a brook and trusted God to take care of him. God did take care of him, sending ravens to feed him morning and night.

The drought continued, and the brook dried up, but Elijah didn't panic. God had a plan that involved a poor widow in the town of Zarephath.

It's not known if the widow had previous knowledge of or faith in the God of Israel. We do know, however, that she lived in the heart of the land of Baal worship, the religion with which Israel had become infatuated and for which Israel was being punished. In fact, at that time, Sidon, the region in which Zarephath lay, represented the forces of evil aligned against God's people.

Whatever the widow believed, she chose to obey the prophet Elijah. She gave up her last bit of food, did as Elijah requested, and was rewarded by having all the food she, Elijah, and her son needed.

Later, when the widow's son grew ill and died, Elijah was apparently still staying with her. The woman assumed that her son's death was a result of some sin she had committed and that Elijah's presence in her house had alerted God to her sin. So she blamed Elijah.

The child's death was an opportunity for God to lead the widow a step further in her faith journey. Her first response to her son's death was to lash out at God by lashing out at Elijah, God's prophet. The Bible doesn't state that God commanded Elijah to raise the child from the dead. But Elijah had faith that God intended this child to live. Acting on this faith, Elijah cried out to God, and God brought the child back to life. This is the first instance recorded in the Bible of someone being raised from the dead.

The widow's response revealed her true trust in God. Elijah demonstrated his powerful faith, and as a result, the widow believed in God. Yet God's people, the people of Israel, remained unfaithful, worshipping the pagan god Baal.

Getting Started

What I've Got

As students arrive, ask each to find a partner. Give each pair a pencil, a calculator, and a copy of the "Let's Go Shopping!" handout (p. 82).

SAY **Have you ever wondered what it would be like to try to provide for your family with very little money? Today you're going to get the chance to see how well you would do. Imagine this: You're at the grocery store, and you've got <u>thirty-five dollars</u> to feed your family for the next two weeks. You've narrowed the number of items you need to the list on the handout I've just given you. The problem is, the total cost of all of these items is more than fifty dollars. With your partner, decide which items to buy.**

Give pairs time to look over their shopping lists and make their decisions. When they're ready, have each pair join another pair to discuss their choices.

SAY **Now that you've made your decisions, you've got another big decision to make. You still need the items on your shopping list. I'd like your new group of four to come up with three ways to get the items that you can't afford to purchase.**

Give foursomes time to think of ideas. When they've finished, have them share their ideas with the rest of the class.

ASK • **What was more difficult: choosing the right items to buy or deciding how to get the groceries you couldn't afford to buy?**
• **What should we do when we can't afford to buy the things we need?**
• **How does trusting God help us when we can't afford things?**
• **What does it mean to trust God completely?**

SAY **Trusting God completely isn't always easy, but it is essential. We can trust God to meet our little needs as well as our big ones. Today we'll talk about how we can trust God for everything we need.**

Bible Story Exploration

A Widow's Trust

SAY **Sometimes trusting God is our only choice. And, in those moments when we truly trust God, he does amazing things.**

Last Week's Impact

As teenagers arrive, greet them warmly, and ask follow-up questions to review last week's study and Key Verse. Ask questions such as "How did you obey God last week?" and "Did you suffer any consequences as a result of rebelling against God last week?"

If you used the Faith Journal option last week, take this time to return your students' index cards to them.

For Extra Impact

Display local grocery stores' newspaper ads. Give students shopping lists without prices. Give students fifteen minutes to find the items on their lists without spending more than thirty-five dollars.

Teacher SkillBuilder

Teenagers are constantly being told what they need. They're bombarded with marketing messages dictating every aspect of their appearance. Their friends constantly discuss the latest fashions and fads.

At the same time, teenagers have a very real need for affection but are often unsure of how to get it. They also need to belong, and some will do almost anything to be part of the in crowd.

As a result, teenagers struggle with differentiating between real and perceived needs. To help them identify their real needs, try these ideas.

• Take them to places in your city where underprivileged people live.

• Show them videos of people who live in poverty.

for OLDER teenagers

Have older teenagers read the Bible story, then simply ask them each to write a journal entry from the widow's perspective. When they've finished, have students read their journal entries to the rest of the class.

Let's read about a woman who trusted God and witnessed a miracle.

Ask students to form groups of four and read 1 Kings 17:7-24.

SAY **Now read the passage again, but this time read it with the idea of disproving it. Analyze the miraculous or unbelievable aspects of the passage, and do your best to disprove the story.**

Give each foursome a sheet of newsprint and a marker for recording their ideas. When everyone has finished, have students gather in the center of the meeting room, and ask each foursome to present its ideas. Ask the following questions after each group's presentation.

ASK • **How well did this group disprove the miracle described in the story?**
• **What could have improved this group's argument?**

After all the foursomes have presented, have students form pairs with students from other groups. Ask teenagers to discuss these questions with their partners.

— Write answers on board —

ASK • **Why do you think the widow was willing to trust God?**
• **How do you think she reacted when she realized that she always had food to eat?**
• **How do you think you would have reacted if you had experienced this miracle?**
• **How did this woman trust God?**
• **What does it mean to trust God completely?**

Instruct students to return to their original foursomes and to exchange the arguments they'd written on newsprint with another foursome. Each foursome should now have a new list of arguments against the miracle described in 1 Kings 17:7-24.

SAY **Read the arguments you've just been given. Then consider them from the widow's perspective, and write the widow's response to each argument.**

Give foursomes time to record their ideas. When they've finished, have foursomes present their ideas.

ASK • **How do we know when God provides for us in a miraculous way?**
• **Is it easy or difficult to disprove the miracles that God does in our own lives? Explain.**
• **Why is it important to trust God's ability and desire to provide for us?**
• **What does it mean to trust God completely?**

SAY **We often take God's provision for granted, or we give the credit to ourselves or others. But the truth is, every time our needs are met, it's because God is providing for us.**

Simple Study in Trust

SAY The widow in this story demonstrated a simple trust in God. She had plenty of reasons to question God. In fact, she was ready to die after her last meal. But she seemed to know that Elijah's words were from God. So she chose to trust God, and that trust carried her through. Let's read a Bible passage to discover the effects of that kind of trust.

Instruct everyone to find a partner, and give each pair a sheet of newsprint and a marker. Ask students to read the Key Verses, Matthew 6:31-33, focusing on verse 31. Have pairs discuss these questions.

ASK
- In what ways do you express worry about what you'll eat or drink?
- In what ways do you express worry about what you'll wear?
- If you trust God, does that mean you'll never think about how you look or what you'll eat? Explain.

SAY Understanding and applying this verse can be difficult for a really materialistic person. Think about the questions or objections a materialistic person would raise while reading this passage.

Give pairs time to think of questions and objections, then ask them to present their ideas.

ASK
- How easy or difficult is it to really trust God for your food and clothes?
- Why is it important to trust God for these things?
- What happens if we don't trust God to meet our needs? Does he still provide for them?

Ask pairs to read Matthew 6:33.

ASK
- What does it mean to "seek first [God's] kingdom and his righteousness"?
- How do we show that we're seeking God first?

SAY It's one thing to trust God to provide for you. It's another to actually seek God's kingdom in everything you do. Think about how you might present this passage to a group of your peers, then make notes of what you would say to them.

Give pairs time to write their ideas. When everyone is ready, give each pair a chance to share its ideas with the class.

ASK
- Is it easy or difficult to explain what it means to seek God's kingdom?
- What difficulties do we face when we seek God's kingdom?
- When is it the most difficult for you to seek God's kingdom?

For Extra Impact

If you know someone who's been homeless and has a testimony about it, this would be an excellent time to have him or her speak to your students about trusting God.

Tip From the Trenches

If your group is small, consider having students work alone to create their lists, then have them form pairs and read their lists to their partners.

- How does seeking God's kingdom before anything else affect a person's life?
- Is it possible for everyone to seek God's kingdom?
- What does it mean to trust God completely?

SAY It's often easier to talk about trusting God than it is to actually trust him. So what do we need to do? We need to fight the battle every day, recognizing that the ability to trust God is itself a gift from God! When we trust God, he will do amazing things in our lives. God will provide abundantly, just as he provided for the widow.

Bible Application

Extreme Trust

SAY You've explored what it means to seek God's kingdom before considering your needs. Now I'd like you to spend a moment telling God about your needs.

Have students each find a place where they can be alone. Give everyone a sheet of paper and a pen. Instruct students to list their needs. Students might list material needs, such as clothes, and intangible needs, such as love or acceptance. When they've finished, have students each find a partner with whom to share their lists.

SAY Now choose one or two needs that you want your partner to pray about with you. I'd like you to incorporate the Key Verses into your prayers for each other. For example, you might pray this for your partner: "Lord, please help Shelly to be patient as you provide for her. Your Word says that we're to seek your kingdom first. Help Shelly to seek your will for her life first and to trust that you will provide for all of her needs."

As students are praying, place a jar at the front of the meeting room. When students have finished praying, invite them to come forward and place their papers in the jar as a symbol of their commitment to trust God to provide for their needs. Finally, ask students to stand in a circle around the jar. Lead a prayer encouraging students to concentrate on seeking God's kingdom in their lives.

After the study, be sure to destroy the papers in the jar.

Faith Journal

Give each student an index card and a pen. Have teenagers write their names and their answers to the following question on their index cards:

- Why is it important to trust God completely?

After teenagers have written their responses, ask them to return the cards to you. Before you meet with the group again, take time to write personal

Tip From the Trenches

To carry this idea through the week, have students commit to contacting each other midweek to ask about the status of their commitments.

for Younger teenagers

Have younger teens write their needs on inflated balloons. After they've prayed, ask students to stomp their balloons as a symbol of their commitment to trust God to meet all their needs.

responses to your students on their index cards. You may want to keep a notebook or a box containing copies of these index cards as well as brief notes of prayer concerns and needs your students share using this assessment tool.

For more information about the Faith Journal option, refer to page 5 of the Introduction.

Tip From the Trenches

To help strengthen the connection between church and home, photocopy the "Taking It Home" page at the end of this study, and either distribute copies to students before they leave or mail them to their homes. Encourage students to complete the reading, activities, and discussion with their families during the coming week.

Let's Go Shopping!

You're at the grocery store, and you have thirty-five dollars with which to feed your family for the next two weeks. You've narrowed your list down to the items below. Now you've got to choose what to buy with the money you have. Circle your choices.

Item	Price
Hamburger (2 pounds)	$5.49
Chicken (1 whole)	$6.39
Diapers (package of 16)	$12.76
Baby Wipes	$2.74
Milk	$2.25
Macaroni and Cheese	$.50
Bread	$1.39
Juice	$1.25
Rice	$2.29
Potatoes	$2.99
Lettuce	$1.50
Ketchup	$1.00
Spaghetti Noodles	$1.25
Spaghetti Sauce	$.99
Toilet Paper	$1.25
Dish Soap	$1.53
Laundry Detergent	$4.95

research required

Talking About It

Driving Home the Point:

"Missionary statesman Hudson Taylor had complete trust in God's faithfulness. In his journal he wrote: 'Our heavenly Father is a very experienced One. He knows very well that His children wake up with a good appetite every morning...He sustained 3 million Israelites in the wilderness for 40 years. We do not expect He will send 3 million missionaries to China; but if He did, He would have ample means to sustain them all...Depend on it, God's work done in God's way will never lack God's supply.' "

(Our Daily Bread, May 16, 1992, as quoted in www.sermonillustrations.com)

Talking At Home:

Read Romans 15:13 with your family, and discuss these questions:

- **Why is it important to trust God?**
- **What hinders our trust in God?**

Give each family member two sheets of paper. Ask everyone to draw one need he or she will commit to trusting God to meet this week. (For example, family members might depict safety or food.) Then ask everyone to depict a need that is a bit out of the ordinary, such as an extra hundred dollars to meet financial obligations or a few extra hours of relaxation. Post all of the pictures on the refrigerator, and every night before bed, praise God for the needs he has met and pray for the unmet needs depicted in your family's drawings.

everywhere

[take home]

Serving the Mighty God

1 Kings 18:16-40

10

 KEY QUESTION: Why should we choose to serve God?

 STUDY FOCUS: Teenagers will discover that a personal relationship with God results in a heart that desires to serve him.

KEY VERSES: "I am the Lord your God, who brought you out of Egypt, out of the land of slavery. You shall have no other gods before me" (Exodus 20:2-3).

A Look at the Study

Study Sequence	Minutes	What Students Will Do	Classroom Supplies
Getting Started	15 to 20	**Show Me!**—Create models that demonstrate the meaning of the word "relationship."	Creative materials of various colors, shapes, and sizes; scissors; straight pins; tape; glue
Bible Story Exploration	10 to 15	**Who's the Troublemaker?**—Participate in a choral reading of the paraphrased Bible story.	Bibles, "Who's the Troublemaker?" handouts (pp. 90-91)
Bible Application	10 to 15	**Choose to Serve Him**—Examine daily choices in light of the Key Verses.	Paper, pens
	up to 5	**Faith Journal**—Respond in writing to an aspect of the Key Question.	Index cards, pens

Age-Level Insight

Teenagers are often busy. Many find themselves struggling to stay on top of schoolwork and responsibilities at home. Others juggle extracurricular activities and part-time jobs as well. And on that rare occasion when an empty time slot appears in their schedules, television, the telephone, and video games munch away their minutes. The teenagers you are ministering to may not understand the importance of making time to serve God. Help them realize that when they nurture a personal relationship with God, he will show them how to please him and that in the process of pleasing him, they will thrive.

NOTES

During the time Elijah was staying in Zarephath, Ahab, the king of Israel, was apparently looking for him. Jezebel, Ahab's wife, had been killing prophets who followed God, and we can assume Ahab and Jezebel wanted to do the same to Elijah. A man named Obadiah was in charge of Ahab's palace. Obadiah was a devout follower of God and had hidden some prophets of God from Jezebel to keep them safe.

God instructed Elijah to present himself to Ahab. The drought had grown so severe that Ahab had sent Obadiah to find grass to keep his horses alive because Ahab didn't want to risk a decrease in his military strength. During his search, Obadiah encountered Elijah, who was headed for his meeting with Ahab. The exchange between Obadiah and Elijah is interesting. Elijah wanted Obadiah to tell Ahab that he was coming. Obadiah was afraid to make that announcement for fear that Ahab would think he was in alliance with Elijah and would kill him, especially if Elijah didn't show up as he said he would. But Elijah promised to keep his word, and Obadiah announced the impending visit to Ahab.

It's apparent from Ahab's first words to Elijah that Ahab blamed Elijah for the drought. The crime Ahab accused Elijah of—being a "troubler of Israel"—was punishable by death (see Joshua 7:25). However, instead of ordering Elijah's execution, Ahab listened to Elijah and did what he said because Ahab was hoping Elijah would be able to end the drought.

Elijah's challenge was intended to publicly prove that the God of Israel is the one true God so that the people would turn from their worship of Baal and once again worship God. Elijah wanted to ensure that there could be no doubt of the contest's fairness, so he asked that all 850 prophets of Baal and Asherah be present to plead with their god. Before Elijah's demonstration of God's power, the people refused to commit themselves to either God or Baal (1 Kings 18:21).

After quite some time had passed without a response from Baal, Elijah began taunting the false prophets, revealing his knowledge of existing myths about Baal. Their response to Elijah's taunts was to cut themselves, a common practice in the pagan worship of those days. People believed that injuring themselves would convince their gods that they were sincere and deserved a response.

When it was his turn, Elijah once again wanted to ensure that the contest couldn't possibly be seen as slanted in God's favor. That's why he had the altar and sacrifice drenched with water. Baal was thought to be the god of water and fire; Elijah wanted to show that the God of Israel is the one true God. When God responded as Elijah knew he would, the people made the right choice. With the people on his side, Elijah took advantage of the moment and got rid of the false prophets, and Ahab didn't stop him. God proved his power and then released the rain to end the drought in Israel.

Getting Started

Show Me!

Set out materials that will inspire teenagers' creativity. Choose items of various colors, shapes, and sizes, such as containers, boxes, plastic foam, yarn, modeling clay, wooden dowels, and toothpicks. Also provide scissors, tape, glue, straight pins, and any other "essentials" you have on hand. Ask students to work in pairs to create a model that demonstrates the meaning of the word "relationship."

Allow students five to ten minutes to work, then gather everyone for show and tell.

ASK
- **In today's culture we hear a lot about relationships, but what does that concept actually mean?**
- **What are some advantages of a personal relationship?**
- **How can we benefit from a personal relationship with God?**
- **Does God benefit from a personal relationship with us? How?**
- **Why should we choose to serve God?**

Bible Story Exploration

Who's the Troublemaker?

Ask teenagers to turn to 1 Kings 18:16-40 in their Bibles. Have students read the passage aloud, each person reading a verse at a time. Distribute copies of the "Who's the Troublemaker?" handout (pp. 90-91). Assign three students the following parts:

- Narrator

- Ahab

- Elijah

Explain that the girls will read together all the parts marked "All the People" and the guys will read together the parts marked "Prophets of Baal." Give students a few minutes to study the handout before beginning the choral reading.

Prompt students to perform the reading, reading their assigned parts.

ASK
- **Why do you think Elijah was so passionate about demonstrating God's power?**
- **How do you think Elijah's established relationship with God affected him during this experience?**
- **How do you think this incident affected Elijah's relationship with God?**
- **Why do you think Elijah chose to serve God in this way?**
- **Why should we choose to serve God?**

Last Week's Impact

As teenagers arrive, greet them warmly, and ask follow-up questions to review last week's study and Key Verses. Ask questions such as "How did you trust God last week?" and "What needs did God meet for you?"

If you used the Faith Journal option last week, take this time to return your students' index cards to them.

for Younger teenagers

Create an atmosphere that will help younger teenagers feel eager to tackle the abstract thinking needed to create their models. Decorate your meeting room with posters, photos, and groups of items that demonstrate various aspects of the word "relationship." For example, you could display pictures of family members and friends interacting, scenes showing interdependence in nature, or groupings of stuffed animals leaning against each other for support.

For Extra Impact

Provide simple costumes, props, and sets to help teenagers dramatize the interaction between Elijah and the prophets of Baal. Or give each student a hat that will designate the character he or she is impersonating.

SAY A relationship with God can inspire us to serve him. As we experience God's love, faithfulness, and grace in our lives, those experiences should drive us to respond by wanting to serve God. When he has done so much for us—even though he owes us nothing—how can we not respond in gratitude and service?

Bible Application

Choose to Serve Him

Distribute paper and pens, and ask teenagers to list all of the decisions they've made from the time they woke up this morning until the present moment. Here are some examples: deciding to hit the snooze button on their alarm clocks, choosing what to eat for breakfast (or choosing not to eat breakfast), choosing what to wear, and choosing who to be with at various times throughout the day.

ASK • How does your relationship with God affect your daily decisions?
• How might your decision-making change as your relationship with God grows?

Ask students to form three groups, then have each group memorize a phrase from the Key Verses, as follows:

• Group 1: "I am the Lord your God"

• Group 2: "who brought you out of Egypt"

• Group 3: "out of the land of slavery."

When students have memorized their assigned phrases, have each group form a line and hold hands. Then have the three lines form one circle. Ask groups to recite their phrases in order: (Group 1) "I am the Lord your God," (Group 2) "who brought you out of Egypt," (Group 3) "out of the land of slavery." Have students continue to recite their phrases in order until the entire verse flows smoothly. Then have everyone say together, "You shall have no other gods before me" (Exodus 20:3).

Challenge teenagers to successfully recite the Key Verses and their reference. Ask volunteers to offer sentence prayers honoring the Lord God.

Faith Journal

Give each student an index card and a pen. Have teenagers write their names and their answers to the following question on their index cards:

• How will you focus on the Lord and serve him daily?

After teenagers have written their responses, ask them to return the cards to you. Before you meet with the group again, take time to write personal responses to your students on their index cards. You may want to keep a notebook or a box containing copies of these index cards as well as brief notes of prayer concerns and needs your students share using this assessment tool.

For more information about the Faith Journal option, refer to page 5 of the Introduction.

Tip From the *Trenches*

Never assume that you know a teenager's reading capability. Some students who are intellectually gifted may have trouble with reading and may feel embarrassed about that "deficiency," while teenagers who seem slow to catch on may be avid readers!

Tip From the *Trenches*

To help strengthen the connection between church and home, photocopy the "Taking It Home" page at the end of this study, and either distribute copies to students before they leave or mail them to their homes. Encourage students to complete the reading, activities, and discussion with their families during the coming week.

Who's the Troublemaker?

NARRATOR: King Ahab went to meet the prophet Elijah.

AHAB *(to Elijah)*: Is that you, you troubler of Israel?

ELIJAH *(to Ahab)*: I have not made trouble for Israel, but you and your father's family have! You've abandoned the Lord's commands, and you've followed worshippers of the false god Baal. Now summon the people from all over Israel to meet me on Mount Carmel. Bring with you the 450 prophets of Baal. And bring the 400 prophets of the goddess Asherah, who eat at Queen Jezebel's table.

NARRATOR: So Ahab sent word throughout all Israel and assembled the prophets on Mount Carmel. Then Elijah went before the people.

ELIJAH: I am the only one of the Lord's prophets left, but Baal has 450 prophets! Get two bulls for us. Let the prophets of Baal choose one for themselves, and let them cut it into pieces and lay it on wood. But do not set the wood on fire. I will prepare the other bull and lay it on wood, but I will not set fire to it. Then you call on the name of your god, and I will call on the name of the Lord. The god who answers by fire—he is God!

ALL THE PEOPLE: What you say is good!

NARRATOR: So the prophets of Baal chose their bull and prepared it for sacrifice. Then they called on the name of Baal.

PROPHETS OF BAAL: O mighty Baal, answer us and send down fire to consume this sacrifice that we are offering to you!

NARRATOR: The prophets shouted to Baal from morning 'til noon, but nothing happened.

PROPHETS OF BAAL: Watch us dance around your altar; hear us cry out in your name. Accept our sacrifice, O mighty Baal!

NARRATOR: But nothing happened. No one answered.

research
required

(continued)

ELIJAH: Maybe you should shout *louder*. Perhaps Baal is deep in thought or busy or traveling. Maybe he's sleeping and must be awakened!

NARRATOR: The prophets of Baal shouted louder. They slashed themselves with swords and spears until their blood flowed. Frantically, they continued prophesying until evening came. But nothing happened. No one answered. No one paid attention.

ELIJAH: Come here and watch, all you people of Israel! I'm taking twelve stones—one for each of the tribes descended from our ancestor Jacob, and I will use them to rebuild the altar of the Lord. See, I am digging a deep trench around the altar that will hold about thirteen quarts of seed. And I'm piling on the wood and arranging the pieces of the bull on the altar. Now I want you to fill four large jars with water and pour the water over the offering and on the wood.

ALL THE PEOPLE: But the wood and the offering will not burn!

ELIJAH: Just do as I said, and not only that! Fill the jars with water a second time and a third time. Pour water until the altar is soggy and the trench is filled!

ALL THE PEOPLE: OK, Elijah, but the wood won't burn.

NARRATOR: So the people followed Elijah's instructions. When it was time for the evening sacrifice, Elijah stepped forward and prayed.

ELIJAH: O Lord, God of Abraham, Isaac, and Israel, let it be known today that you are God in Israel and that I am your servant. I have done all these things at your command. Answer me, O Lord! Answer me so that all these people will know that you are God and that you are turning their hearts back to you, O Lord!

NARRATOR: Suddenly the fire of the Lord fell and burned up the sacrifice. And it burned not only the sacrifice; it burned up the wood, the stones, and the soil, and it licked up the water as well! When the people saw this, they fell down with their faces to the ground.

EVERYONE: The Lord—he is God!

research required

Talking About It

Driving Home the Point:

"For every man the music of hope is found in Jesus Christ."

(Richard Lee, *Issues of the Heart*)

Talking At **Home:**

Read Matthew 25:35-46 with your family. Make a list of projects that you can do together to serve the Lord. Think about your neighborhood, your community, your country, and your world. Then discuss these questions:

- **How is helping other people like serving Jesus himself?**
- **What will Jesus say to those who have helped others?**
- **Which family projects on your list include helping people in need?**

take home everywhere

God Is Always With Us

1 Kings 19:9-18

11

God Speaks to Elijah in a Whisper

 KEY QUESTION: When we feel alone, how can we know God is with us?

 STUDY FOCUS: Teenagers will recognize the benefits of focusing on their Savior rather than on their circumstances.

KEY VERSE: "So do not fear, for I am with you; do not be dismayed, for I am your God. I will strengthen you and help you; I will uphold you with my righteous right hand" (Isaiah 41:10).

A Look at the Study

Study Sequence	Minutes	What Students Will Do	Classroom Supplies
Getting Started	10 to 15	**How Does That Sound?**—Imitate sounds and guess their sources.	Paper bags, paper, scissors, pen
Bible Story Exploration	10 to 15	**What Are You Doing Here, Elijah?**—Read the Bible story and record impressions from Elijah's perspective.	Bibles, "Elijah's Spiritual Journal" handouts (p. 98), "Elijah's Journey" handouts (p. 99), pens
	10 to 15	**What Am I Doing Here, Lord?**—Reflect on their focus in life.	Bibles, newsprint, marker, tape
Bible Application	15 to 20	**Spiritual Handprints**—Record God's "handprints" on their lives.	Bibles, colored paper, markers, staplers, newsprint, tape
	up to 5	**Faith Journal**—Respond in writing to an aspect of the Key Question.	Index cards, pens

Age-Level Insight

With so much going on in the world around them, teenagers may have difficulty focusing their thoughts. Some students have mastered this skill in lower grades as a result of activity and interest centers in the classroom, where they were able to practice concentrating despite the "organized chaos" around them. But many people (adults as well as children and teens) can't quite get a grip on this important capability. In the spiritual realm, it may seem especially hard for some students to focus on the reality of our invisible God. Challenge teenagers to "see" the Lord in creative ways and to become aware of his divine "handprints" on their lives.

NOTES

When Ahab told Jezebel what had happened to the false prophets on Mount Carmel, she was furious and vowed to kill Elijah within twenty-four hours. Even though Ahab had witnessed God's power on the mountain, he apparently did nothing to oppose her. Elijah ran for his life.

Elijah's fear of Jezebel may seem strange to us. But remember that no human is perfect. After the events on Mount Carmel, Elijah may have been physically and emotionally exhausted. Rather than relishing another chance to prove God's power over Jezebel, he tired of the fight. Or maybe he was disappointed or angered that his life was still in danger after all God had done to prove that he is God. He may have been overwhelmed by the prospect of having to do spiritual battle again right away. Whatever the reason, he felt he had had enough and retreated into the desert. Even though Elijah's faith was apparently weak at this point, God was faithful and brought food and drink to him in the desert. In fact Elijah hadn't abandoned God; after eating and drinking, he began a forty-day journey to Horeb, the mountain of God.

Elijah's statement recorded in 1 Kings 19:10 reveals his feelings. He felt alone, abandoned by the Israelites, and tired of running and hiding to protect his life. It seemed to him that he was the only one in all the world who truly followed God. Elijah shared his feelings with God, and God responded by promising to bless Elijah with his presence.

God's lesson to Elijah in all that happened on the mountain may have been in response to something we're not told. Elijah apparently wanted God to judge Israel through a terrifying event such as a mighty wind, an earthquake, or a fire. But God wanted Elijah to know that those kinds of judgment weren't part of his plan at that time. Rather, in coming to Elijah in a gentle whisper, God showed Elijah that he wanted him to continue his mission of speaking to the Israelites for him. And Elijah was reminded that God was with him even when he felt utterly alone.

After demonstrating his presence, God again asked Elijah what he was doing there (1 Kings 19:13). By responding exactly as he had the first time, Elijah showed that he didn't really understand the significance of what had just happened to him. Even so, God continued to lead Elijah on his mission, knowing that Elijah would eventually understand the lesson of the events he'd just experienced.

After giving Elijah instructions for his next move, God had some encouraging news to keep Elijah going: Seven thousand others in Israel hadn't worshipped Baal; Elijah wasn't alone in following God. So Elijah was assured not only that God was beside him when he felt alone, but also that thousands of others in Israel were faithful to God. He would never *really* be alone.

Getting Started

How Does That Sound?

Prepare small, paper "sound sacks"—one for each group of five that you anticipate. Cut ten one-inch strips of paper for each sack. On each paper strip write one of the following words or phrases:

- sheep
- cow
- lawn mower
- can opener
- parrot
- rooster
- bumblebee
- mosquito
- worried parent
- crying baby

Form groups of five, and give each group a sound sack. Ask one person in each group to pull a strip of paper out of the group's sack and imitate the sound written on it. Tell students that when the others guess the sound, the sack will be passed to another group member and the game will continue until the sack is empty.

SAY **Today we're going to continue our study of some amazing experiences in the life of the prophet Elijah. To understand how Elijah felt during one particular episode in his spiritual journey, we'll need to imagine some specific sounds that he heard while spending the night in a mountain cave. But before we begin, I'd like you to identify a few more interesting sounds.**

ASK • **For example, has any one of you ever heard the sound of fear?**

Watch facial expressions and call on teenagers who are likely remembering a sound that caused them to feel fearful. If teenagers decline to share, don't force or tease them. Simply move on to someone else.

- **What about loneliness? How does loneliness sound?**
- **When you feel alone, how can you know God is with you?**

Last Week's Impact

As teenagers arrive, greet them warmly, and ask follow-up questions to review last week's study and Key Verse. Ask questions such as "How did you serve God last week?" and "How does it feel to help someone in need?"

If you used the Faith Journal option last week, take this time to return your students' index cards to them.

For Extra Impact

Before the meeting, tape-record eight to ten different noises that teenagers commonly hear throughout the day. Here are some examples: a ringing alarm clock, a popular radio host, teeth being brushed, a parent's urgent voice calling, "Don't be late!" and feet running up and down stairs. Play the individual sounds, challenging teenagers to guess the source of each noise.

Tip From the Trenches

If you have access to a word processor and printer, you can save time and energy by typing the sound sources onto a full sheet of paper. Then cut the strips with a paper cutter or scissors.

Bible Story Exploration

What Are You Doing Here, Elijah?

Ask students to remain in their small groups and to open their Bibles to 1 Kings 19:9-18. Distribute pens and copies of the "Elijah's Spiritual Journal" handout (p. 98), then have students read the journal entries and follow the printed instructions. Allow about five minutes for students to complete the journal activity, then gather teenagers into one group.

ASK • **Why do you think God said what he did to Elijah after his forty-day journey?**
• **From Elijah's answer in verse 10, what can we learn about Elijah's thoughts? What was he focusing on?**

SAY **God understood Elijah's situation. He knew the answers to every question that was racing through Elijah's agitated mind. And God knew how to handle this frightened, overwhelmed man.**

ASK • **Elijah stood at the mouth of the cave and responded to God. What does this response in verse 14 tell us about Elijah's focus?**

SAY **By disrupting Elijah's pity party, Elijah's heavenly Father was encouraging Elijah to focus on the Savior rather than the situation.**

Give everyone a copy of "Elijah's Journey" (p. 99). The map shows the area described in 1 Kings 19—from Damascus in the north, to Mount Sinai (also called Mount Horeb) at the southern tip of the Sinai Peninsula. Ask students to trace Elijah's journey as they call out the sites mentioned in the Scripture: from Mount Carmel to Jezreel to Beersheba to Mount Horeb (Mount Sinai), then north to Damascus.

ASK • **Why do you think God told Elijah to travel back the way he came?**
• **When we feel threatened as Elijah did, where does God want us to focus?**
• **When we feel completely alone, as Elijah did, how can we know that God cares and is watching over us?**

What Am I Doing Here, Lord?

Before the study, write the following questions on a sheet of newsprint, and post the newsprint where everyone can see it:

• How would you respond if the Lord asked you, "What are you doing here?"

• Where is your focus when you feel threatened or afraid?

• How can you know that God is with you when you feel alone?

Have students find a quiet place in the meeting room, separated from everyone else, and spend time thinking about their responses to these questions.

Don't play music or talk with other adult leaders during this time. Try to keep the atmosphere as quiet as possible. After about ten minutes, ask teenagers to gather in their original groups of five to look up Isaiah 41:10 in their Bibles and share their thoughts.

Bible Application

Spiritual Handprints

SAY **Journaling is one method you can use to remind yourself that God is with you. By recording occasions when you're aware of his goodness or writing about times you're feeling alone or dismayed, you'll eventually learn to recognize the Lord's handprints on your life.**

Provide various colors of paper (or white if that's the only color available), fine line markers, and staplers. Give each student ten sheets of paper, and ask everyone to trace his or her handprint on each sheet. Then have students staple the sheets together to make a writing pad for recording the "spiritual handprints" they observe in their daily lives.

Ask teenagers to copy the Key Verse, Isaiah 41:10, from their Bibles onto the front page of their journals. Write the following discussion starters on a sheet of newsprint, and as they finish the project, ask individuals to form small groups and talk about them:

• a time you felt God's comforting presence when you were frightened

• a time you remembered God's awesome power when you felt dismayed

• a time you felt strengthened by God's "righteous right hand"

Faith Journal

Give each student an index card and a pen. Have teenagers write their names and their answers to the following question on their index cards:

> • **What can you do to remind yourself that God is with you continuously?**

After teenagers have written their responses, ask them to return the cards to you. Before you meet with the group again, take time to write personal responses to your students on their index cards. You may want to keep a notebook or a box containing copies of these index cards as well as brief notes of prayer concerns and needs your students share using this assessment tool.

For more information about the Faith Journal option, refer to page 5 of the Introduction.

Tip From the Trenches

Make sure teenagers understand the meaning of "dismay" as they read the Key Verse. Tell them that dismay is not just a feeling of sadness. Dismay may result when someone senses the possibility of serious conflict or danger, and it can cause a person to lose confidence and courage.

for Younger teenagers

Explain to younger teenagers that there are many ways to journal. If they prefer not to write sentences or phrases, they may draw pictures or create a code to make recording in their journals more fun.

Tip From the Trenches

To help strengthen the connection between church and home, photocopy the "Taking It Home" page at the end of this study, and either distribute copies to students before they leave or mail them to their homes. Encourage students to complete the reading, activities, and discussion with their families during the coming week.

Elijah's Spiritual Journal

[think]

Monday:

Queen Jezebel has vowed to take my life. I'm feeling afraid and vulnerable. Must run for my life!

Tuesday:

I'm sitting under a broom tree in Beersheba. Oh Lord, I'm so tired and discouraged. I've had enough. Take my life!

Wednesday:

An angel of the Lord has provided me with baked bread and a jar of water. I'm feeling strengthened by the food. Must continue to flee, or Jezebel will fulfill her threat to kill me!

Forty days later:

Have been traveling for almost six weeks now, running from Queen Jezebel to the mountain of God. Found a cave where I will spend the night. Feeling exhausted and dismayed.

Read 1 Kings 19:9-18. Imagine what Elijah thought and felt while he was inside the mountain cave. Then, in your own words, continue writing in Elijah's journal.

Night in a cave:

_____

_____

_____

_____

_____

_____

research required

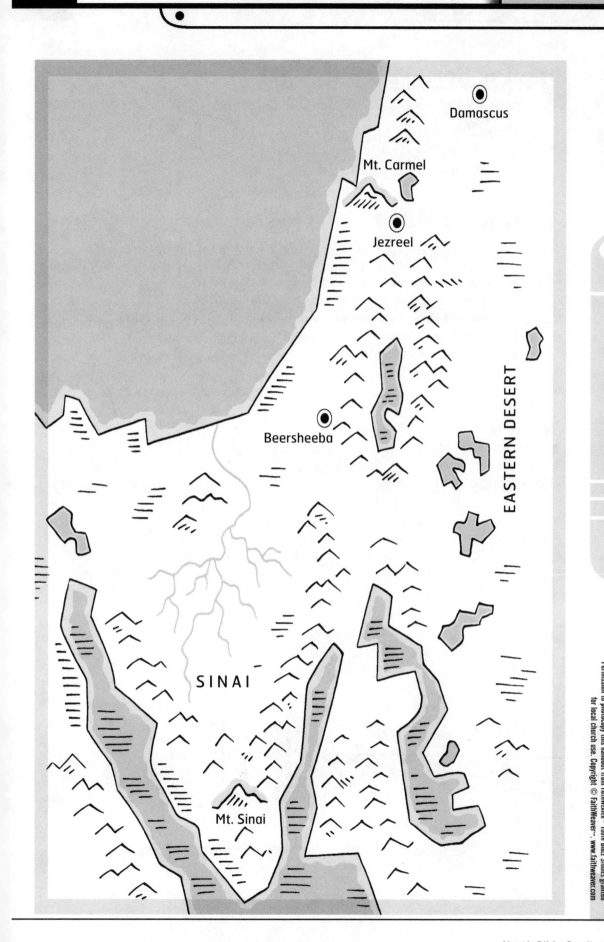

Damascus

Mt. Carmel

Jezreel

EASTERN DESERT

Beersheeba

SINAI

Mt. Sinai

[think]

research required

everywhere

take home [everywhere]

Driving Home the Point:

"Even though it may *seem* like you stand in the gap alone, you really don't. Jesus promised He'd always be with us! There are times you'll stand humanly alone, but there is *never* a time when He's not with you!"

(Susie Shellenberger, *Rock Your World*)

Talking At Home:

Read Deuteronomy 31:1-12 with your family, and discuss these questions:

- **When you think about the Lord God, how do you feel?**
- **When we feel alone, how can we know God is with us?**
- **Why do you think we sometimes feel God's presence and other times feel as if God is nowhere to be found?**
- **How do we experience God's presence?**

Ask each family member to take a turn reading aloud Deuteronomy 31:6. Think about God's command to be strong and courageous. How can remembering God's words help your family to be strong during difficult times?

Faithful Friend

2 Kings 2:1-15

12

God Takes Elijah to Heaven

 KEY QUESTION: What does it mean to be faithful?

 STUDY FOCUS: Teenagers will examine faithfulness in light of their friendships.

KEY VERSE: "So whether you eat or drink or whatever you do, do it all for the glory of God" (1 Corinthians 10:31).

A Look at the Study

Study Sequence	Minutes	What Students Will Do	Classroom Supplies
Getting Started	10 to 15	**True Friends**—Explore the meaning of faithful friendship.	"For a True Friend" handouts (pp. 106-107), pens, newsprint, marker, tape
Bible Story Exploration	15 to 20	**Elisha Loses His Faithful Friend**—Create "freeze frames" of each scene in the Bible story.	Bibles
	5 to 10	**Overcoming Obstacles**—Study the Scripture to find obstacles to Elisha's faithfulness, then compare them with obstacles in their own lives.	Bibles, newsprint, marker
Bible Application	10 to 15	**A Test of True Friendship**—Make a list of activities they enjoy with friends, then apply the Key Verse to determine which activities demonstrate faithfulness to God.	Paper, pens
	up to 5	**Faith Journal**—Respond in writing to an aspect of the Key Question.	Index cards, pens

Age-Level Insight

Friendship and faithfulness are topics of great importance to teenagers but are especially crucial to young people who don't have many friends and who find it difficult to place trust in their peers. As you work with teenagers, take care not to make promises that you may not be able to keep. Make every effort to respect students equally. And help all teenagers realize that when imperfect people let them down, they can depend on our faithful God to love them unconditionally.

NOTES

After God chose Elisha to succeed Elijah as prophet in Israel, Elisha immediately became Elijah's attendant. Ahab and Jezebel continued in their evil ways, and Elijah pronounced God's judgment on them. Eventually Ahab was killed in battle and was replaced as king of Israel by Ahaziah. Ahaziah ruled only two years before he died, having been punished by God for consulting Baal instead of God (2 Kings 1:16-17). Joram succeeded Ahaziah as king.

We don't know how Elisha knew what was about to happen, but apparently he realized that his mentor, Elijah, would soon be taken to heaven. Elisha was totally committed to staying with Elijah until the very end.

We know of three companies of prophets that existed during the days of Elijah and Elisha. It appears that Elijah visited each of these companies one last time before he was taken to heaven. Elijah's suggestion that he go on without Elisha after visiting each of these places may have been intended to test Elisha's faithfulness. Or perhaps Elijah merely wanted to be alone. Elisha, however, refused to forgo his last hours with Elijah. He wanted to benefit as much as possible from Elijah before Elijah went to be with God. Elisha's persistence was rewarded when Elijah asked what he could do for Elisha before he was taken to heaven.

Elisha's request for a double portion of Elijah's spirit was likely based on inheritance rules of the day, which entitled the oldest son to a double portion of his father's estate. Elisha, succeeding Elijah as prophet in Israel, wanted that double portion of God's power to help him face his responsibilities as spiritual leader of the nation.

God had supported and protected Elijah throughout his ministry. Now, as Elisha witnessed the heavenly host, in the form of a chariot of fire and horses of fire, take Elijah home to God, Elisha was allowed to see God's spiritual forces at work. The whirlwind and fire were signs of the power and presence of God.

Elijah was the second person in the Old Testament to never experience death. As with Enoch before him, he was simply taken to heaven (Genesis 5:24; Hebrews 11:5).

Elijah had thrown his cloak around Elisha's shoulders when he first called Elisha to join him (1 Kings 19:19). After Elijah ascended to heaven, Elisha picked up Elijah's cloak, symbolizing Elisha's full assumption of Elijah's ministry. Elisha tested how fully the power of God was with him—and demonstrated it to all who could see—when he parted the water of the Jordan by striking it with the cloak. Elisha had been faithful to Elijah and to God, and God rewarded him with the strength he would need to minister as a prophet amid the evil conditions that existed in Israel.

Getting Started

True Friends

ASK • **How would you define a faithful friend?**

As teenagers share their thoughts, encourage input from each age level to achieve a well-balanced definition.

ASK • **How can you know if you are a faithful friend?**

Form groups of six to eight, and give everyone a "For a True Friend" handout (pp. 106-107). As you give students pens, tell them not to write their names on their handouts.

SAY **I'd like you to think about what you would and would not be willing to do for a true friend. Write a word or phrase in the first blank on your handout. Then pass the handout to someone else in your group. That person will answer the questions "Would you?" and "Why or why not?"**

After teenagers have completed the first box of the handout, ask them to pass the handouts again so that a different person within their small group fills in the "I would not" box. For example, Teen A writes, "I would tell a secret to a true friend" then passes the handout to Teen B, who answers yes or no to the "Would you?" question and answers the question "Why or why not?" Teen B then passes the handout to Teen C, who fills in the blank following "I would not." Teenagers continue writing and passing the handouts until all the blanks are filled.

As groups are working on the handout, write the following discussion questions on a sheet of newsprint, and post it where everyone can see it:

- What does it mean to be faithful?

- What must a person do to prove that he or she is a true friend?

- What is the value of a friend who is truly faithful?

When groups have completed the handout, ask a few volunteers to share what has been written on their handouts. Then direct students' attention to the questions posted on the wall, and encourage students to discuss them in their groups. Allow five minutes for discussion before asking volunteers to share their thoughts.

Bible Story Exploration

Elisha Loses His Faithful Friend

Ask students to form six groups, and assign the following Scripture references:

- Group 1—2 Kings 2:1-3 (Elisha remains with Elijah as he travels to Bethel.)

- Group 2—2 Kings 2:4-5 (Elisha remains with Elijah as he travels to Jericho.)

Last Week's Impact

As teenagers arrive, greet them warmly, and ask follow-up questions to review last week's study and Key Verse. Ask questions such as "Did you face fear or dismay last week? How did you deal with those emotions?" and "How many divine handprints did you notice?"

If you used the Faith Journal option last week, take this time to return your students' index cards to them.

Tip From the Trenches

Some teenagers may find the instructions for this activity too complicated. You may simplify the process by asking students to sit together in a circle. Distribute the "For a True Friend" handout, and give instructions for the "I would" statement. When everyone has finished writing, ask students to pass their papers to the person on their left, and give instructions for the "Would you?" and "Why or why not?" questions. When everyone has finished writing, have students pass their papers again. Continue this step-by-step process until all the blank spaces on the handout have been filled.

for OLDER teenagers

Have older teenagers share their thoughts about whether a man and woman should be faithful friends before they consider marriage.

• Group 3—2 Kings 2:6-7 (Elisha remains with Elijah as he travels to the Jordan River.)

• Group 4—2 Kings 2:8-10 (The Jordan River divides after Elijah strikes the water with his cloak. Elisha asks for a double portion of Elijah's spirit.)

• Group 5—2 Kings 2:11-12 (Elijah is taken to heaven in a whirlwind. Elisha grieves.)

• Group 6—2 Kings 2:13-15 (The spirit of Elijah rests on Elisha.)

SAY **Each of these references represents a scene in the Bible story. With your group, study the verses you've been assigned, then create a "freeze frame" of that scene, using your bodies, your facial expressions, and anything else in the room that you decide will be helpful. Think of your freeze frame as a living photograph that represents a scene from the lives of Elijah and Elisha.**

Choose one person in your group to direct and position everyone else. You'll have five minutes to prepare, then we'll meet together to read the Bible story and illustrate it with the freeze frames you've created.

When everyone is ready, ask the student directors to prepare to read the verses their freeze frames depict. Ask members of Group 1 to assume their freeze-frame positions, then ask their director to read 2 Kings 2:1-3. As Group 1 is seated, repeat the process with Group 2, and continue in this manner until all the groups have presented their freeze frames.

Overcoming Obstacles

SAY **Three times Elijah said to Elisha, "Stay here." And each time Elisha responded, "I will not leave you."**

ASK • **What does that tell you about their relationship?**
• **What does it tell you about Elisha's relationship with God?**

SAY **Elisha had to overcome several obstacles in order to remain faithful to God. I'd like you to examine the entire Bible story to identify the people and circumstances that may have seemed to Elisha like roadblocks in his journey.**

Have students form groups of three and search 2 Kings 2:1-15 for the obstacles Elisha had to overcome. Here are some examples:

• In verses 3 and 5, he was pressured by the prophets.

• In verses 2, 4, and 6, he chose to disagree with his friend.

• In verse 12, he mourned because Elijah had been taken from him.

• In verses 14 and 15, he had to decide whether to continue to serve God.

Allow four to five minutes for teenagers to examine the Bible story. Then ask each trio to identify one obstacle. List all of the suggestions on a sheet of newsprint.

ASK • Which of these obstacles have you experienced?
• Do any of these roadblocks obstruct your friendship with God? Which ones?
• What does it mean to be faithful to God?

Bible Application

A Test of True Friendship

Give everyone a sheet of paper, and instruct teenagers to fold the paper in half lengthwise. On the left side of the paper, ask teenagers to make a list of activities they enjoy with their friends. Allow several minutes for students to compose their lists.

ASK • How can a person have fun with friends and still be faithful to God?

Read the Key Verse aloud with your students:

SAY "So whether you eat or drink or whatever you do, do it all for the glory of God" (1 Corinthians 10:31).

ASK • What does that mean, "whatever you do, do it all for the glory of God"?
• How can you glorify God and still have fun with your friends?

Ask teenagers to read the activities they've listed and to ask themselves, "Am I being faithful to God when I do this?" Ask students to write their answers on the right side of the fold, then have them spend a few minutes sharing their thoughts with the other members of their trios.

Ask students to stand, form a circle, and join hands. Ask them to repeat the Key Verse in unison once more, and encourage spontaneous student prayer.

Faith Journal

Give each student an index card and a pen. Have teenagers write their names and their answers to the following question on their index cards:

• **What can you do to nurture faithful friendships?**

After teenagers have written their responses, ask them to return the cards to you. Before you meet with the group again, take time to write personal responses to your students on their index cards. You may want to keep a notebook or a box containing copies of these index cards as well as brief notes of prayer concerns and needs your students share using this assessment tool.

For more information about the Faith Journal option, refer to page 5 of the Introduction.

For Extra Impact

Photograph the freeze frames, then display the photos in the meeting room. This will especially benefit small groups, since all the teenagers will have been involved in creating the scenes and there will therefore have been no audience.

Teacher SkillBuilder

Don't ever be afraid to adapt a curriculum or an idea to fit your group. Too often leaders try to use a study as is, even though it may not be appropriate to their settings or groups. Other leaders reject the idea of using curriculum because it seems to lock them in to leading a study in a specific way.

But why reinvent the wheel—or in this case, the study? If a curriculum or an idea doesn't fit your group, use it as a springboard for your own ideas. You know best what will work with your group.

Tip From the Trenches

To help strengthen the connection between church and home, photocopy the "Taking It Home" page at the end of this study, and either distribute copies to students before they leave or mail them to their homes. Encourage students to complete the reading, activities, and discussion with their families during the coming week.

For a True Friend

I think

I would _____ a true friend.

Would you? _____ Why or why not? _____

_____.

• *change my hair color for*

• *keep a secret for*

I would not _____ a true friend.

Would you? _____ Why or why not? _____

_____.

• *give money to*

• *betray*

research
required

I would _____ a true friend.

Would you? _____ Why or why not? _____

_____.

• *break up with my girlfriend for*

I would not _____ a true friend.

Would you? _____ Why or why not? _____

_____.

(continued)

I would _____ a true friend.

Would you? _____ Why or why not? _____
_____.

• loan my car to

• lie to

• do homework for

I would not_____ a true friend.

Would you? _____ Why or why not? _____
_____.

• go to a movie with

• have a drink with

research required

[t h i n k]

KEY VERSE:

"So whether you eat or drink or whatever you do, do it all for the glory of God"

(1 CORINTHIANS 10:31).

take home everywhere

Driving Home the Point:

"I've learned that there is no reason to play games with God, pretending everything is okay between you and Him...He invites you to have a relationship with Him. That is the blessed assurance of faith."

(Mac Powell, "Finding the 'Blessed Assurance' " in *City on a Hill*)

Talking At Home:

Read Psalm 91:1-2 with your family, and ask family members to talk about times they've experienced a deep sense of peace. Discuss these questions:

- **How does faith in God help us to feel at peace?**
- **What can we do to show the Lord that we appreciate his protection and love?**

God Protects His People

2 Chronicles 20:1-30

13

Jehoshaphat Trusts God for Victory

 KEY QUESTION: What should we do when we have problems?

 STUDY FOCUS: Teenagers will be encouraged to put their problems into perspective and trust God with all of their concerns.

KEY VERSE: "Cast all your anxiety on him because he cares for you" (1 Peter 5:7).

A Look at the Study

Study Sequence	Minutes	What Students Will Do	Classroom Supplies
Getting Started	10 to 15	**Quick! Do Something!**—Imagine they are faced with imminent danger and decide how to defend against attack.	Timer, newsprint, marker
Bible Story Exploration	15 to 20	**King Jehoshaphat's Big Problem**—Read the Bible story and analyze the king's battle plan.	Bibles, paper, pens
	10 to 15	**Wise Words**—Scan the Scripture for wise words that may help with problem solving.	Bibles, paper, pens, mini–poster boards, colored markers
Bible Application	10 to 15	**The Anxiety Battle**—Discuss how anxiety can affect decision making and problem solving.	Bibles, newsprint, marker
	up to 5	**Faith Journal**—Respond in writing to an aspect of the Key Question.	Index cards, pens

Age-Level Insight

The teenage years are typically filled with problems that must be solved and decisions that must be made. Older teenagers are challenged to sort out problems that arise when they learn to drive, begin dating, and enter the workplace. They must look toward the future and make decisions concerning college, career, and marriage goals. Younger teenagers often have problems with parents, siblings, and peer pressure. Throughout puberty even the smallest inconvenience can seem life threatening! Remain open to the Holy Spirit's leading as you guide and counsel teenagers. And let the Lord love them through you.

NOTES

The events in this passage occurred at about the same time that Elisha succeeded Elijah as Israel's prophet. Jehoshaphat was the king of Judah at about the same time that Ahab was the king of Israel. God was with Jehoshaphat in his early days as king because he followed God and didn't worship Baal. Jehoshaphat's father, Asa, had done much to return the people of Judah to the worship of God, and Jehoshaphat followed in his footsteps. Because of God's blessing, Jehoshaphat grew powerful. Leaders of the lands around Judah sought his favor by bringing him gifts (2 Chronicles 17:1-13). The number of fighting men available to Jehoshaphat was astounding—over a million men, according to 2 Chronicles 17:14-18.

When Jehoshaphat learned of the threat of a vast army invading from Edom, he didn't respond by sounding the battle cry and mustering his troops. Rather, he went to the Lord to discover what God wanted him to do. This king was a man who had his priorities right!

God responded to Jehoshaphat's prayer through Jahaziel. His message must have been tough to accept. How could they win a battle without fighting? But Jehoshaphat responded in faith and encouraged his fighting men to meet their enemies without initiating the fighting.

At that time it was not unusual for soldiers to go into battle shouting and chanting war cries. However, Jehoshaphat's commandment was different. Instead of trumpeting their own strength or courage, his soldiers were to summon God's help through their praise and worship.

In the ambushes described in 2 Chronicles 20:22-23, the allied armies coming against Judah apparently began fighting one another in the confusion of battle. This event is similar to the victory God provided Gideon and his three hundred men against the Midianite army (Judges 7:22).

After God won the battle for them, the armies of Judah carried off the plunder of war; then they gathered specifically to praise God for the victory. When they returned to Jerusalem, they went immediately to the Temple to praise and worship God there.

The fear of God came upon the surrounding countries, and Jehoshaphat and Judah were rewarded with rest as a result of their obedience. This pattern persists throughout Chronicles: Kings who were obedient to God experienced victory and peace, while those who were disobedient experienced turmoil and defeat. Those who turned to God had their problems solved. Those who turned away from God simply created more problems for themselves.

Getting Started

Quick! Do Something!
Get everyone's attention.

SAY We've just received word that a vast army is surrounding our community. These soldiers have come from the other side of the sea and are waging war against American imperialism. We have five minutes to prepare for their attack.

Choose one student who can handle a leadership role.

SAY [Student's name], I'm putting you in charge. Tell us what we need to do.

Allow about five seconds of silence for the student leader to process what you've just said and to adjust to the idea that he or she is now the center of attention. Immediately set a timer for five minutes.

SAY We have five minutes. Our lives are at stake. What can we do to avoid being slaughtered?

Now stand back and watch what happens. If the student leader accepts the challenge and takes charge of the situation, don't interfere. If the student leader is overwhelmed by the challenge (which is likely if the group is large) and doesn't take control within ten seconds, call out the names of several other students and say, "Quick! Do something. We don't have much time!"

When the timer sounds, gather everyone for debriefing.

SAY Time's up. The vast army from the other side of the sea is here.

ASK • What are we going to do?

Call on the student leader(s) to summarize what, if anything, has been decided. Then ask for voluntary comments from other students. If you have observed noteworthy behavior on the part of individual teenagers, ask those students for their advice.

Form groups of four. Display the following questions on a sheet of newsprint, and ask students to discuss them in their foursomes.

• How did you feel during this activity?

• If you had been the designated leader, what would you have done?

• If a serious and unexpected problem were to arise, what should we do?

Allow time for students to interact, then get everyone's attention.

ASK • Are there places in our world right now where attacks like the one we've just imagined could actually happen? Where?

- How do you think the people in those countries would perceive our daily problems?
- What should we do when we have problems? ?

Bible Story Exploration

King Jehoshaphat's Big Problem

Ask the groups of four to divide into pairs. Distribute paper and pens, and have teenagers turn in their Bibles to 2 Chronicles 20:1-30.

SAY King Jehoshaphat had a big problem. When he found out about it, he was alarmed. However, as you'll see as you read the Scripture, the king didn't let that delay his decision making. He knew immediately what to do.

Have pairs read the entire Bible story together and make notes about King Jehoshaphat's battle plan. Allow about ten minutes, then get everyone's attention.

ASK
- What do you think of the way King Jehoshaphat handled his problem?
- How would you have reacted if you were one of the king's subjects?
- If you had been in the king's position, what actions would you have taken to protect your kingdom?
- Do you think your solution would have been as effective as the king's? Why or why not?

Wise Words

Have teenagers return to their original groups of four. Provide foursomes with paper and pens. Ask them to review the Bible story to find and paraphrase encouraging words that might be helpful when they're solving problems and making decisions.

Here are some examples:

- Resolve to inquire of the Lord (verse 3).
- Seek the Lord's help (verse 4).
- Remember that power and might are in God's hand (verse 6).
- Remember to keep your eyes on the Lord when you don't know what to do (verse 12).
- Don't be afraid or discouraged; remember that the battle is God's, not yours (verse 15).
- Face the problem; the Lord will be with you (verse 17).
- Sing to the Lord and praise him (verse 21).

Provide mini-poster boards and colored markers. Have teenagers make

for Younger teenagers

To help younger teenagers understand what you mean by "Jehoshaphat's battle plan," display the following outline:

- When the king learns about the problem, what is his first response?
- Who does he ask for guidance?
- What actions does the king take? Why?

Teacher SkillBuilder

Christian parents and teenagers face many obstacles in their efforts to understand each other. Power struggles, disagreements, and defiance have been known to strain even the healthiest family relationships in Christian homes. It's even tougher, though, for teenagers whose parents don't know the Lord. As you guide students through this study, keep in mind that Satan loves to cause trouble in homes where teenagers are thriving. Be sensitive to special circumstances in the life of each student, and remember that there are always two sides to stories of trouble between teenagers and their parents.

locker-sized posters using one or more of the phrases they've found. Give students the option of either making their own posters or working together to create one poster in each foursome.

Allow about ten minutes, then call on individuals to share their posters and encouraging words.

Bible Application

The Anxiety Battle

SAY **Think about the feelings you experienced during the first activity, and call out words that identify them.**

As teenagers think of words to label their emotions, write them on a sheet of newsprint.

ASK • **How can anxiety influence decision making and problem solving?**

Have teenagers turn in their Bibles to 1 Peter 5:7. Ask a student to read the Key Verse: "Cast all your anxiety on him because he cares for you."

ASK • **What does God's Word say about handling problems?**
• **When we have a problem, what should we do first?**

Ask a student to write the Key Verse on a sheet of newsprint, using the New International Version. Have students read the verse together several times. Finally, spend a few moments in prayer, asking God to help students remember to turn to him first when they have problems.

Faith Journal

Give each student an index card and a pen. Have teenagers write their names and their answers to the following question on their index cards:

• **How will sharing your problems with God help you solve them?**

After teenagers have written their responses, ask them to return the cards to you. Before you meet with the group again, take time to write personal responses to your students on their index cards. You may want to keep a notebook or a box containing copies of these index cards as well as brief notes of prayer concerns and needs your students share using this assessment tool.

For more information about the Faith Journal option, refer to page 5 of the Introduction.

for OLDER *teenagers*

Give older teenagers the opportunity to share specific personal problems and to pray for one another in pairs or foursomes.

Tip From **the Trenches**

Be prepared to offer teenagers practical alternatives to anxiety. Here are a few suggestions:

• Spend thirty minutes relaxing; listen to music or take a hot bath.

• Close your eyes. Inhale slowly and deeply. Exhale slowly.

• Keep reminders of God's love and power close at hand in the form of posters, bookmarks, stickers, and friends who are devoted to honoring the Lord.

• Don't allow yourself to think negative, unflattering thoughts.

• Seek God's guidance, comfort, and peace.

Tip From **the Trenches**

To help strengthen the connection between church and home, photocopy the "Taking It Home" page at the end of this study, and either distribute copies to students before they leave or mail them to their homes. Encourage students to complete the reading, activities, and discussion with their families during the coming week.

Taking It Home

take it home! everywhere

Driving Home the Point:

"Many Christians are convinced there's less to God than meets the eye. Though they would never admit it, their theology owes more to *The Wizard of Oz* than to the Bible. Behind God's booming voice and powerful deeds is a little man pulling levers. They suspect this is true of God because they know it's true of themselves."

(Tim Woodroof, *Walk This Way*)

Talking At Home:

Read John 16:33 with your family, then discuss these questions:

- **Have you ever felt embarrassed or hurt because of your faith in Christ?**
- **What does Jesus promise in this verse?**
- **How do these promises encourage people who love and serve the Lord?**

As a family, watch for evidence of God's peace during the upcoming week. Agree to show one another the peace sign—even in public places—as you experience God's peace.

Evaluation of Group's FaithWeaver™ Bible Curriculum
FaithWeaver Youth Bible Studies

Please help us continue to provide innovative and useful resources for ministry by taking a moment to fill out and send us this evaluation.

•   •   •

The things I like best about this quarter of curriculum are:

This quarter could be improved by:

Curriculum I used before using FaithWeaver was:

I will use FaithWeaver in future quarters (circle one):

Not Likely				**Definitely**
1	2	3	4	5

How many youth were in your class this quarter?_____

How many age levels in your church used FaithWeaver this quarter? _____

Optional Information:

Name _____

Street Address _____

City _____State _____ Zip _____

E-mail_____

Please mail or fax your completed evaluation to:

Group Publishing, Inc.
Attention: FaithWeaver Feedback
P.O. Box 481
Loveland, CO 80539
Fax: (970) 679-4370

Thank you!

More FaithWeaver™ Youth Bible Studies

Check out the other titles available in the FaithWeaver Youth Bible Studies series. All of the lessons address relevant youth ministry issues and draw from Bible passages that strengthen students' faith in God. Each of these 13-session leader guides includes reproducible student pages.

Real Life: Creation, The Fall, Noah, Abraham

ISBN 0-7644-0911-5

Got Jesus?: Get Ready, Get Born, Get Called, Get Surprised

ISBN 0-7644-0938-7

Pure Power: The Word, The Cross, The Spirit, The Church

ISBN 0-7644-0957-3

Pursuing God: Jacob, Joseph, Moses Israel *(formerly God Chasers)*

ISBN 0-7644-0984-0

God at Work: God Delivers, God Provides, God Commands, God Wins

ISBN 0-7644-1004-0

Jesus Live!: Coming Soon, A Star Is Born, The Main Event, The Road Show

ISBN 0-7644-1026-1

Outrageous Obedience: Gideon, Samson, Hannah, David

ISBN 0-7644-1080-6

It's A Boy: Birth Announcements, Baby Shower, Licensed to Teach, Making His Mark

ISBN 0-7644-1206-X
(available September 2001)

Order today from your local Christian bookstore, online at www.faithweaver.com or write:
Group Publishing, P.O. Box 485, Loveland, CO 80539-0485.

Exciting Resources for Your Youth Ministry

At Risk: Bringing Hope to Hurting Teenagers

Dr. Scott Larson

Discover how to meet the needs of hurting teenagers with these practical suggestions, honest answers, and tools to help you evaluate your existing programs. Plus, you'll get real-life insights about what it takes to include kids others have left behind. If you believe the Gospel is for everyone, this book is for you! Includes a special introduction by Duffy Robbins and a foreword by Dean Borgman.

ISBN 0-7644-2091-7

All-Star Games From All-Star Youth Leaders

The ultimate game book—from the biggest names in youth ministry! All-time no-fail favorites from Wayne Rice, Les Christie, Rich Mullins, Tiger McLuen, Darrell Pearson, Dave Stone, Bart Campolo, Steve Fitzhugh, and 21 others! You get all the games you'll need for any situation. Plus, you get practical advice about how to design your own games and tricks for turning a *good* game into a *great* game!

ISBN 0-7644-2020-8

The Youth Worker's Encyclopedia of Bible-Teaching Ideas

Here are the most comprehensive idea books available for youth workers. With more than 365 creative ideas in each of these 400-page encyclopedias, there's at least one idea for every book of the Bible. You'll find ideas for retreats and overnighters...learning games...adventures...projects...affirmations...parties... prayers... music...devotions...skits...and more!

Old Testament   ISBN 1-55945-184-X
New Testament   ISBN 1-55945-183-1

Awesome Worship Services for Youth

These 12 complete worship services involve kids in 4 key elements of worship: celebration, reflection, symbolic action, and declaration of God's Truth. Flexible and dynamic services each last about an hour and will bring your group closer to God.

ISBN 0-7644-2057-7